In My Feelings

A TEEN GUIDE TO DISCOVERING WHAT YOU FEEL

SO YOU CAN DECIDE WHAT TO DO

Vidal Annan Jr., Ph.D.

free spirit

PUBLISHING®

Library of Congress Cataloging-in-Publication Data
Names: Annan, Vidal, Jr., author.
Title: In my feelings : a teen guide to discovering what you feel so you can decide what to do / Vidal Annan, Jr., Ph.D.
Description: Huntington Beach, CA : Free Spirit Publishing, an imprint of Teacher Created Materials, [2023] | Includes index. | Audience: Ages 12 & up
Identifiers: LCCN 2022048675 (print) | LCCN 2022048676 (ebook) | ISBN 9798885540001 (paperback) | ISBN 9798885540049 (ebook) | ISBN 9798885540056 (epub)
Subjects: LCSH: Emotions in adolescence¬—Juvenile literature. | Teenagers¬—Mental health¬—Juvenile literature. | BISAC: YOUNG ADULT NONFICTION / Social Topics / Emotions & Feelings | YOUNG ADULT NONFICTION / Health & Daily Living / Mental Health
Classification: LCC BF724.3.E5 A56 2023 (print) | LCC BF724.3.E5 (ebook) | DDC 155.5/124¬—dc23/eng/20221026
LC record available at https://lccn.loc.gov/2022048675
LC ebook record available at https://lccn.loc.gov/2022048676

Edited by Christine Zuchora-Walske
Cover and interior design by Colleen Pidel

Printed in China

Free Spirit Publishing
An imprint of Teacher Created Materials
9850 51st Avenue North, Suite 100
Minneapolis, MN 554442
(612) 338-2068
help4kids@freespirit.com
freespirit.com

FSC
www.fsc.org
MIX
Paper | Supporting
responsible forestry
FSC® C144853

Dedication

To my loved ones, who have always encouraged and supported me in living out my values.

Acknowledgments

There is one name on the cover of this book, but in no way is this the work of just one person. If not for the kindness, openness, and support of many others, the book would not exist. First I would like to thank my parents, who encouraged me to follow my dreams. In their eyes, nothing was beyond my ability to accomplish. I needed every ounce of that belief to write this book. Many thanks also to my wife, Nana, who put up with me being absorbed in my thoughts, my notes, and my laptop screen for the last six years. Her understanding, love, and support gave me the strength and confidence to keep working. Thanks to my siblings, who responded with excitement every time I mentioned the book or updated them on each step of the publishing process. To the Free Spirit team, especially Christine Zuchora-Walske and Amanda Shofner, who shared my enthusiasm for this subject and shepherded me, a novice, through the many steps of editing and publication. Many thanks to Dr. Erica Miller, who many years ago introduced me to acceptance and commitment therapy (ACT). I was intrigued by this approach at the time, but I had no idea how much it would change my understanding of clinical theory and practice. As any discerning clinician will notice, ACT processes lie at the core of this book. To Robert Constant, who agreed to meet with me years ago to discuss the development of my book. He wrote a wonderful book himself, so his insights were invaluable to me. I remember his enthusiastic feedback when I shared my book title with him. His reaction gave me the turbocharge I needed to keep grinding. I would also like to acknowledge the hundreds, if not thousands, of teenagers I have worked with over the course of my career. Each one of them taught me a lesson about human suffering and resilience. By sharing their emotional lives with me, they gave me the data I needed to hopefully help them. And finally, thank you to my two teenage children! Watching them grow and live out their values has been the joy of my life. They continue to impress and influence me with every step they take in their lives. May they forever listen to the message in their emotions (even if they don't listen to me).

Contents

Introduction

If you are a teen who has picked up this book by your own choice, thank you. I appreciate you taking the time to learn an important skill on your journey to adulthood: understanding your emotions. I have worked with teens for most of my career as a clinical psychologist, and despite what some adults may say about you and your peers, I know that you are in fact interested in learning and growing. Your choice to read this book shows that you are.

If you didn't choose this book yourself, but someone is encouraging you to read it, I thank you too! The person who gave you this book—hopefully a caring adult—probably sees promise in you and knows that with the right information, you can take your life to the next level. This book is for you as well.

Regardless of why you are reading this book, it will help you better understand the feelings that you are having and use them to set and reach your goals. As a teenager, you are likely experiencing new feelings or old feelings in new ways. And you are probably trying to figure out what the heck is going on inside you!

Whether your feelings are pleasant (such as love, joy, or excitement) or unpleasant (such as loneliness, anxiety, or envy), you're trying to decipher them and determine what to do with them. This is a normal part of being a teen. I hope as you read on, you will see that emotions are more than just weird feelings you have in reaction to situations. They are important bits of information about yourself, others, and the world that you can understand and use to your benefit.

> Emotions are more than just weird feelings you have in reaction to situations. They are important bits of information about yourself, others, and the world that you can understand and use to your benefit.

At its core, this book is about emotional intelligence. Emotional intelligence refers to how smart you are about emotions. It describes how well you interpret, manage, and make use of feelings in your life.

People with high emotional intelligence are often good at understanding their own and others' feelings and making helpful or useful decisions based on this emotional information. Some people think emotional intelligence may be more important for a successful life than cognitive intelligence, the ability to learn, remember, reason, and solve problems. Emotional intelligence isn't something you either are or aren't born with; you can learn and develop it.

That's where this book comes in. I wrote it to help you improve your emotional intelligence—especially one of its key elements, emotional self-awareness. Emotional self-awareness is your ability to recognize a feeling you're experiencing, label it correctly, and then figure out what it means to you and your current situation. Let's say you have to make a decision, and your stomach is tight, your heart is racing, and your hands are sweaty. What would you call the emotion you're feeling? It does not feel great, and maybe you'd like it to go away, but could you study this feeling to better understand it and use it to help you decide what to do?

The answer is yes. But sometimes emotions are hard to figure out. In fact, many adults still struggle with this process! But with a little help, you can learn to be more emotionally aware.

This book is designed to be read by teenagers like you. Caring adults may get their hands on this book and use it to understand and help you, but I'm not talking to them; I'm talking to you. This book is meant to interest *you* and give *you* information you can use right away. It's organized so you can find what you need easily. The first four chapters explore what it means to be a teenager, what emotions are, and why you have them. The following eight chapters delve into specific, individual emotions that you may be experiencing daily. You don't need to read this book from front to back unless you want to. Please feel free to jump right into the chapter of your choice! You can read some or all of this book and read it in whatever way helps you get the information you need to understand your feelings and use them to improve your life.

CHAPTER 1
The "Emotional" Teen

This book is about emotions—specifically, emotions experienced during the teen years. Compared to other stages of human development, these years tend to bring more intense emotional experiences. Movies, music, literature, and other forms of art and media are filled with images and stories of teens displaying strong feelings. These characters are often portrayed as absorbed in and overwhelmed by their feelings, to the point of disregarding their own and others' well-being. Whether feelings are pleasant or unpleasant, they may seem to dominate the lives of teenagers and dictate their actions and choices. The teen years aren't actually that turbulent, but people your age do experience new emotions, along with old emotions in new ways. These emotions are a natural result of all the changes that happen when you're a teen—in your body, school, family, relationships, and other areas of your life.

Has an adult ever asked you "What is wrong with you?" or "Why do you act like that?" If so, and if you find such questions annoying, it might help to remember that often these adults just want to understand and maybe help you. You may shrug or answer "I don't know" because you truly *don't* know what's wrong or why you did something. You're simply trying your best to adjust to all the changes that seem to be happening to you all at once. The constant flurry of feelings can leave you wondering "Who am I?" and adults wondering "Who are you?"

As a clinical psychologist, I often have the opportunity to talk with teens at moments when they are open and vulnerable about their feelings. In therapy, they may let down their guard and show that they are struggling to figure out their lives. One of the strategies I use as a therapist is helping teens become more emotionally self-aware. When they're experiencing a range of feelings, it is valuable to identify those feelings and explore them to gain more information.

WILL'S STORY

One teen I worked with, Will, faced a unique and puzzling social problem. He felt confident and comfortable around strangers, but nervous around people he knew well, such as close friends and teammates. He could not understand why. "Isn't it usually the other way around?" he asked me. After all, he pointed out, most people are comfortable with familiar folks and nervous around new ones. He described being able to talk easily with people he'd recently met. He could introduce himself, talk about his interests, and ask friendly questions. But when it came to calling a longtime friend to hang out, he would find himself freezing up, overthinking the situation, and sometimes talking himself out of it. This was becoming a problem because on weekends, if his friends did not reach out to him, he was often home alone feeling bored. Will and his parents were starting to think there was something wrong with him. Did he have some kind of strange mental disorder that was affecting his social behavior?

After listening closely to Will and thinking about it for a while, I realized that he was confused about what feelings he was having and what they meant. I thought that if he could identify his feelings, it might change how he felt about himself and his experience. First I gave Will's feeling a name. His face showed surprise and relief when I used the word *anxious* to describe his experience. He seemed happy that his emotion had a name and that it wasn't *crazy* or *weird*. I explained that anxiety is a natural human response to uncertainty and doubt. As you will see in chapter 7, anxiety is an emotion that warns you when you might be in danger of an emotional wound, like rejection. In Will's case, when he wanted to invite friends over, he would often start to think about whether they *really* wanted to hang out with him or might agree to come over just to be nice. Maybe he was bothering them, he thought, and they had better things to do. If these thoughts were true, it could mean that his buddies didn't actually like him. That's what really worried him. His anxiety around potential social rejection was more intense with friends than with strangers because the rejection of friends would be more painful. With strangers, there was no serious emotional investment, so a rejection would not hurt as much.

As we talked, I could see Will gradually relax. Now that his feeling had a name, it also had *meaning*. He started to understand that his emotion was not just a "bad" feeling messing up his social life and his mental health, which therefore had to be "treated" in therapy. Rather, his anxiety was reflecting how close he felt to his friends and how much their opinions mattered to him. Of course, identifying the emotion and increasing his understanding was not the end of the story. He still had to figure out how to invite his friends over when he wanted to. But he became much more open to finding solutions once he had some emotional self-awareness.

Will's experience is just one example of the emotional challenges teenagers may face. He will probably have more confusing and bewildering situations to figure out, but he has an advantage now. If he does feel anxiety again, he will likely recognize it, call it by name, understand what caused it, and be able to use this knowledge to make good decisions.

Most people do not know why emotions exist or what purpose they serve for humans. Everyone has emotions, but they don't come with a user's manual to help people understand what causes them or help people figure out what to do with them. Most of the time, emotions just seem to happen to you. You might feel like you are a victim of your emotions. This can be particularly challenging when you are a teen. You are in the midst of important life changes and may still be coming to grips with them. Strong emotions may leave you feeling powerless and uncertain. You may also feel that others have a much better handle on their feelings. (This isn't usually true, by the way.)

Tackling Emotional Challenges with Emotional Intelligence

Although emotions have no user's manual, knowledge on the topic is vast and growing. Scientists have been hard at work for many years trying to figure out what emotions are, why humans have them, and how they affect people. This is critical work because people who are knowledgeable about emotions in themselves and others have an advantage in the quest for personal and social success. In other words, people who are more emotionally aware tend to connect more effectively with others, make better decisions, and feel less "crazy" when dealing with stressful situations. Scientists describe someone's level of emotional awareness as their *emotional intelligence*. They say that emotional intelligence is just as important to successful human functioning as cognitive intelligence is.

Emotional intelligence is the ability to recognize, control, and use emotions for effective decision-making. It's made up of five basic elements:

- **self-awareness:** the ability to recognize and understand your own feelings
- **self-regulation:** the ability to control your own emotional reactions and express your emotions appropriately
- **self-motivation:** the ability to set and stay committed to goals on your own
- **empathy:** the ability to understand other people's emotions and reactions
- **social skills:** the ability to relate to and engage well with others

People who are more emotionally aware tend to connect more effectively with others, make better decisions, and feel less "crazy" when dealing with stressful situations.

ELLA'S STORY

Ella is an ordinary teenager. Consider the following scenarios from her life:

- Ella's best friend gets upset when she hangs out with other friends.
- Ella's younger brother always seems to be angry at her.
- Ella shared some important news with a friend, who responded, "I don't care."
- Ella feels like throwing up every time she takes a test in school.
- Ella's boyfriend doesn't post photos of them together on social media.
- Ella can wake up on time for soccer practice but not for school.

What is Ella's brother's problem? Why isn't her boyfriend posting photos even though she does? And those exams—ugh!

* * * *

These scenarios are very confusing if you don't understand the emotions that motivate them. Imagine if Ella had some insight into her brother's anger or her best friend's jealousy. Would she be able to handle the situations better? She probably would—and that is the benefit of emotional intelligence.

Emotional intelligence isn't inborn. It is a skill that anyone can learn by taking the time to study and practice it. This means that if you struggle to understand and make use of emotional information or deal with emotional change, you can improve! You can learn how to better recognize emotions in yourself and others and use that information to reach personal goals and build stronger relationships.

In fact, now may be the best time to learn about emotions. As a teen, you can vividly recall the simpler feelings from your childhood as you begin to experience the more complicated range of emotions that you'll take with you into adulthood. You also are intellectually mature enough to understand feelings in more sophisticated, abstract ways. You can use these abilities to strengthen your emotional skills and use them to address both current and future challenges.

The Importance of Self-Awareness

This book focuses mainly on emotional self-awareness for two reasons. The first is that self-awareness is the core of emotional intelligence. If you cannot identify and understand your own internal experiences, you will not be able to understand others. There is a Buddhist saying that captures this idea: *To conquer oneself is a greater task than conquering others*. The second reason is, in my experience, most teens can figure out what to do once they figure out what they feel. In other words, it is understanding the emotion that may be your biggest challenge, not necessarily knowing what to do with the emotion. Like Will, you might not have the words to describe your feelings—especially if they are new, unpleasant, or overwhelming. You might know only that you're having a strong emotion and it feels weird. Your actions might be based more on trying to avoid or control the emotion rather than on what you can learn by paying attention to it.

Most teens can figure out what to do once they figure out what they feel.

Emotional self-awareness can be daunting at first because there are so many emotions, each with its own unique experience and function for you as an individual. My goal is to give you basic information about several key emotions so you can recognize them, understand them, and then figure out how to use them to your benefit. If you can tell your feelings apart and have a sense of what each feeling means, you will be in a better position to cope with your emotions and use them wisely.

Imagine, for example, that you and your best friend are both into soccer. You have played together for the past few years, and you both try out for the best team in your town. You find out two weeks later that your friend made the team! You haven't heard yet if you were selected. Your mind begins to race with thoughts of your friend playing on the team without you. Your stomach tightens and your mouth goes dry. Your fists clench and your teeth grit. When your dad asks you what's going on, you can't find the words to answer him. What are you feeling? Envy? Anxiety? Anger? Competitiveness? All of these feelings all at once? What will you do if you don't make the team?

What if you didn't just *know* that you were having difficult thoughts, feelings, and body sensations as you waited for your acceptance or rejection, but also had a deeper *understanding* of those emotions? Some adults say that if they had had a better sense of their emotions when they were younger, they might have avoided difficult situations or handled them better. Emotional self-awareness doesn't necessarily lead to a confusion-free, low-conflict life, but it can make it easier to cope with challenging situations. In the soccer scenario, you may or may not make the team with your friend, but understanding what's going on inside you emotionally may help you seek support from others, stay connected to your friend, and keep striving for your goals.

This book will not cover every single feeling that you will experience in your teen years, but it looks at some of the most common emotions. These are love, anger, sadness, anxiety, and happiness. It also considers other emotions that are sometimes confused with each other, such as envy/jealousy and guilt/shame. But first, let's define two terms that you'll see frequently: *teen-ager* and *emotion*. It will be helpful to understand these two ideas in depth before you consider how they interact.

Thinking About Feeling

Emotional intelligence is a skill you can improve. One way to strengthen this skill is to reflect on times when you have had strong emotions. Think of a time when you felt especially emotional. Do you know what specific emotion you were feeling at the time? Was the emotion pleasant or unpleasant? Did the emotion help you in the situation or make things worse?

CHAPTER 2
Teenagers and Emotions

Who is a teenager? What are emotions? These may seem like dumb questions. A teenager is anyone 13 through 19 years old, and emotions are just feelings that happen to you . . . right? Yes—but there's more to it. Being a teen is not just about your age. It's also about the changes that happen in your life during this period between childhood and adulthood. And emotions are more than random occurrences; they actually play out in a pretty logical way based on your experiences. To understand your emotions, you also need to understand your experiences.

> To understand your emotions, you also need to understand your experiences.

Changes, Changes

Let's take a few minutes to look at the biological, cognitive, and social changes that you may experience on the road to becoming an adult.

Childhood

Before adolescence, children focus on exploring themselves and their immediate environments. Babies start by learning how to control their bodies and communicate with others. Then they move on to finding out what the wider world consists of and how they can interact with it. Young humans learn how to relate to others and the physical world through play. Play also helps kids figure out what they like and don't like as well as what is easier and what is more challenging for them. This self-knowledge is helpful for the next stage—adolescence—when life gets more complicated and individual identity becomes important.

Adolescence

BIOLOGICAL CHANGES

The official starting point of adolescence, or the teen years (even if it happens before age 13), is puberty. During the biological process of puberty, your body matures toward adulthood. Your body releases hormones that cause it to grow rapidly, change shape, become hairier, and develop the ability to reproduce.

COGNITIVE CHANGES

Your brain also changes quite a bit during the teen years. You can think more abstractly, focusing on ideas and concepts beyond what you see, smell, hear, taste, and feel. You are able to reason, meaning that you can look at situations from many different perspectives, use logic, and think through different outcomes. You may feel a strong urge to explore, define, and establish your identity. Your identity is who you think you are across different aspects of your life, including your family relationships, friendships, romantic connections, school, community, and work. Up to this point in your life, your identity has been defined largely by what caregivers, close friends, and relatives think about you. As a teen, you may now want to see what the rest of the world thinks about you—and build your own identity independently.

SOCIAL CHANGES

In addition to mind and body changes, as a teen you'll probably experience many transitions in your social environment, such as at school. You'll move from the relatively sheltered, structured, and supportive world of elementary school to the more competitive, independent, and sometimes image-focused worlds of middle school and high school. In these environments, you will explore relationships in new ways, including romantically. Adults may have higher expectations of your behavior, and your schoolwork may be more challenging. Home expectations may change as well. Your parents may require you to be more responsible—follow rules better, take care of your belongings, and do what is asked of you at school and with friends. These expectations may lead to conflict between you and your parents. You may want independence, but at the same time you may think the responsibilities that come with independence are a hassle.

A WORD ABOUT WORDS

Throughout this book, when I use the word *parent*, I am referring to any adult caregiver or guardian you have in your life—including a biological parent, stepparent, foster parent, grandparent, aunt, uncle, older sibling, or other person.

These biological, cognitive, and social changes are a lot for anyone to go through. The sheer volume of changes may spark quite a range of emotions. The road to independence and adulthood is paved with new feelings and new versions of old feelings. But why do teens feel such a wide variety of emotions and feel them so often? To find the answer, let's first take a look at what emotions are, how they play out, and what purpose they serve.

Defining Emotions

If someone were to ask you to list some emotions, you would probably have no trouble coming up with at least five right away. Given some extra time to think, you could probably list 15 or 20 emotions. Now what if someone were to ask you to explain a specific emotion, such as sadness or disgust or joy? Hmm . . . that might be a bit more difficult. Explaining emotions is no easy task. Since ancient times, philosophers, scientists, and other brilliant thinkers have been trying to get a handle on what is happening when humans experience emotions.

EMOTIONS AROUND THE WORLD

Many cultures have names for emotions that do not translate easily to English. To capture the experience of these emotions in English takes a long description. Here are some examples:

- *Eleutheromania* (Greek)—an intense, irrepressible, manic desire for freedom

- *Gigil* (Tagalog)—the irresistible urge to pinch or squeeze someone because you are overcome with love and affection for them

- *Iktsuarpok* (Inuit)—the anticipation you feel when you're waiting for someone and you keep going outside to check if they have arrived

- *Mbuki-mvuki* (Bantu)—to shed your clothes so you can dance more freely

- *Njuta* (Swedish)—to deeply enjoy, to profoundly appreciate

- *Sukha* (Sanskrit)—genuine lasting happiness that has nothing to do with your circumstances

- *Tizita* (Amharic)—a bittersweet remembrance and longing for a person, thing, or time gone by

- *Yuan bei* (Chinese)—a sense of complete and perfect accomplishment

How many emotions do humans have? Scientists' answers range from as few as four core feelings (happiness, sadness, anger, and fear) to as many as hundreds of emotions. Some of these are likely familiar to you, while others don't even have formal names in English. For example, what do you call that feeling of enjoyment you have when something unfortunate happens to people you dislike? English has no word for this feeling, but German does: *schadenfreude.* It's schadenfreude you might feel when the too-cool basketball player who ignores you at school misses the final shot in the championship game.

Some scientists propose that a small number of primary emotions keep people alive and are universal to all. Primary emotions are generally considered to be the four core emotions plus a few others, such as disgust, surprise, interest, shame, and/or trust. Primary emotions are innate; they happen automatically and quickly, and they are difficult to control. For example, you feel disgust when you see, smell, touch, or taste something that could be poisonous. The gag reflex you may experience when disgusted is your body trying to get rid of something that might be dangerous. According to this theory, primary emotions combine to produce all the other feelings you experience. For example, perhaps fear and disgust combine to create revulsion; sadness and happiness mix to make melancholy; and anger and sadness together form betrayal.

Here's my own definition of emotion. It is based on my study of emotions and my ongoing therapy practice and teaching in a variety of settings:

Emotion *is when you experience a complex pattern of changes in your body and mind in response to an internal or external event. These changes occur simultaneously or nearly so and give you information you can use to understand your world and make decisions.*

My definition packs in a lot of ideas. Let's look at these ideas one by one using the model of an emotion chain reaction.

The Emotion Chain Reaction

What causes emotions? If you can understand what brings on an emotion, you stand a better chance of understanding how you feel so you can name the emotion. Let's skip the complicated neurobiology and focus on what you consciously experience, by looking at a process called the emotion chain reaction. The emotion chain reaction is a series of events that leads to the experience of an emotion.

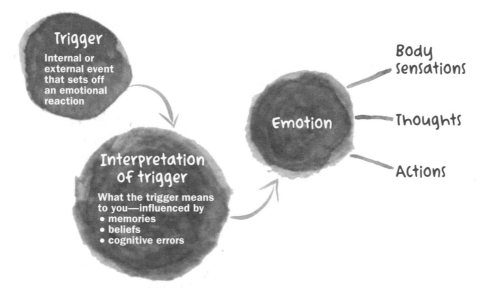

Trigger

A trigger is anything that sets off an emotional reaction. It can be an internal or external event. An internal trigger happens *inside* the body. It could be a thought, sensation, urge, or memory. For example, pain from an injury or a memory of losing a game might trigger emotions such as sadness, anxiety, or anger. Your feelings may arise in response to these experiences inside you. An external trigger, on the other hand, happens *outside* the body. It could be a person, a situation, or a thing. For instance, if you see food you don't like, it may trigger a feeling of disgust.

THE WORD *EMOTION*

The word *emotion* is a fairly recent term, first used in the 1500s. (Yes, that's recent!) Other words that people have used in the past to mean the same thing are *sentiments*, *passions*, and *sympathies*, among others. This book uses the terms *emotions* and *feelings* interchangeably. The modern word *emotion* comes from the Old French word *emouvoir*, which means "to stir up." The French word itself comes from the Latin word *emovere*, which means "to remove, move out, agitate." All these words suggest a movement, an unsettling, or perhaps a disturbance within our being, which is just how emotions often feel.

Interpreting the Trigger

Every trigger is a neutral event in that it can lead to many types of emotions. Which emotion you experience in reaction to a trigger depends on how you interpret, or understand, the trigger. A certain trigger may cause you anxiety because you interpret it as a threat, while it may generate excitement in a friend who interprets it as an opportunity. Your interpretation depends on your past experience and your beliefs.

Past experience, in the form of memories or learned habits, can cause you to view a trigger in a particular way. Let's say you've been scratched by a cat in the past. This memory may cause you to feel nervous around your friend's kitten and want to avoid it. However, if you've had a loving relationship with a pet of your own, you may have more pleasant memories and, as a result, see your friend's kitten as a cute, loving animal that brings joy.

Beliefs are thoughts or perspectives that you hold as true. They too can affect how you interpret a trigger. If you believe you will fail a test because you didn't study, then you might feel panicky at exam time. However, if you believe that you've studied hard, then you may feel confident as you take the test.

You may be thinking that sometimes you are not even aware you are interpreting a trigger. That's correct: the process of interpreting a trigger is not always conscious. Sometimes, it is so quick that you're hardly aware it's happening.

> If you can understand what brings on an emotion, you stand a better chance of understanding it.

Emotion

Emotion is the pattern of body sensations, thoughts, and actions that occur in response to a trigger. It is a natural outcome. You can think of specific emotions as different combinations of sensations, thoughts, and actions. For example, anxiety might be a combination of increased heart rate (sensation), visions of doom and gloom (thoughts), and an urge to run away (action), while sadness may be a combination of low energy level (sensation), notions of loss or inadequacy (thoughts), and an urge to lie down or just not move (action).

BODY SENSATIONS

Emotions almost always express themselves through our bodies. When you're having an emotion, you'll often experience some change in how your physical body is functioning. This could be your visible outer body (arm or leg movements), internal organs (heart or stomach), blood flow, the activity of cells and neurochemicals, or electrical signals in your brain.

For example, your heart may beat quickly when you're excited or scared; your stomach may flip when you're nervous; your face may feel warm when you're embarrassed; your throat may tighten when you're sad; and your forehead may wrinkle when you're confused. The brain is well connected to the rest of the body through the nervous system, so what happens in one part of the body (brain or elsewhere) directly affects other parts.

Charles Darwin, a biologist who lived and worked in the 1800s, wrote a book titled *The Expression of the Emotions in Man and Animals*, in which he focused on facial expression as one of the primary and universal forms of communicating emotions in humans and other animals. Think about the number of facial expressions humans have and how quickly you can detect a feeling based on the changes you see in another person's face. Many scientists since Darwin have extended his studies by studying how people communicate emotions through other physical functions, such as voice and body language.

EMOJIS AND EMOTICONS

The popularity of emojis and emoticons in electronic communications show how important facial expressions and body language are to humans. These little faces and images get emotional messages across quickly and effectively because most people understand them, regardless of the languages they speak.

THOUGHTS

When you have an emotion, it is often associated with a thought. This thought could be words you hear or images you see in your mind. A thought could sound like a voice, or it could be a memory or a fantasy playing out like a video in your imagination. For example, when you're angry at someone, you may think, "I hate that person!" and imagine telling them so. Or if you're feeling affection toward someone, you may hear your internal voice say, "They are so cute!"

ACTIONS

Emotions also have an action component. When you have a feeling, you want to do a certain thing. The action might be as simple as laughing when you're excited, running when you're scared, or crying when you're upset. Or the action might be complicated, such as coming up with a lie when you feel guilty or talking in class when you feel bored. What you do links directly to the emotion you're experiencing. In some cases, the links may be conscious; that is, you are aware of the emotion that causes your action. In other cases, the links may be completely unconscious; that is, you have no idea why you are behaving in certain ways. Another distinction to pay attention to is that sometimes your actions may be voluntary, or under your control, and sometimes they may be automatic, or happening even before you realize what is going on. For example, have you ever heard a loud bang that made you jump? That is an automatic, or involuntary, reaction to fear. On the other hand, a voluntary action in response to the emotion of love for your mom might be to hug her.

LEAH'S STORY

Leah has just started her first job, at a fast-food restaurant. She is excited to finally be making her own money. She considers herself a hard worker and always arrives on time. The part of the job she enjoys the most is interacting with the customers. She likes talking to them and hearing the different combinations of food they order. French fries with coffee—why not? One day she is taking orders from the drive-through, and she hears a voice she recognizes from school. It's Ramon, who is in her French class. Leah has had a crush on him since freshman year but has never said anything to him. As soon as she recognizes his voice, her heart skips a beat. She wants to do everything perfectly and come across as professional and friendly, but also fun and interesting. She will have to see Ramon to give him his food, and she wants to make a good impression. Her heart gallops, and she struggles to remember what Ramon has ordered. She takes a deep breath and tries to calm down and focus. When she opens the window to take his payment and hand over his food, she is thrilled by the grin of recognition on his face. He's as happy to see her as she is to see him! What is more, she gets the order right and makes it through the interaction without fainting or embarrassing herself.

* * * *

Leah was triggered by recognizing Ramon's voice. She interpreted the trigger as both an opportunity to fail and an opportunity to impress. These simultaneous interpretations led her to experience the simultaneous feelings of anxiety and excitement. Her galloping heartbeat may have been a body expression of both feelings. Luckily for Leah, her excitement was stronger than her anxiety, and she was able to stay calm. Ramon's happy reaction was a big payoff for Leah's understanding of her emotions and her effort to choose her actions.

Why You Have Emotions

Now that you know what emotions are, let's explore why you have them. This question is just as challenging to explain as what an emotion is. Here are a few possible answers.

Information

Emotions provide information about yourself, others, and the world. Let's say you move your body in a certain way and feel pain. The pain tells you that part of your body might be injured and that you should be careful the next time you make a similar movement. Other types of physical discomfort, such as hunger, tiredness, and sleepiness, also give you information about your environment and yourself at that moment. In other words, pain provides data you can use to make decisions. Emotions function in the same way. Like physical pain, emotional pain (for example, a feeling such as sadness, disappointment, or anger) triggered by a certain person can help you decide whether to interact further with that person or avoid them.

Focus

Emotions help you focus on something important that's happening. Think about the last time you felt angry at someone. You probably found it hard to concentrate on anything else while you were angry. When you are having a strong feeling, it brings your body sensations, thoughts, and actions into alignment and overrides everything else. This focusing can be seen as a survival asset. Emotions help keep you alive by avoiding danger and bringing you closer to other humans. For example, imagine you are walking in the wilderness. You spot a sudden movement in the grass and jump back in fear. You notice a snake slithering off, startled by your jump. The snake might be poisonous, and you might have stepped on it and been bitten if you hadn't jumped back in fear.

Communication

Emotions help you communicate. This idea goes back to scientists like Darwin, who proposed that emotions are a quick way to project experiences or information to others. When you express emotions, it tells others what is going on with you faster and more easily than using words, and hopefully, this helps others act accordingly. If you have ever seen someone crying and felt sad for them and felt the need to offer some kind words or a hug, that would be an example that supports the idea of emotions as an efficient way to communicate. Through behaviors like crying, laughing, smiling, frowning, jumping, slumping, and sighing, you can let people know that you are experiencing an emotion and whether you need them to come closer or stay away.

Motivation

Emotions move you to act. Some scientists have described emotions as the motivating force for action in human beings. Thoughts may help you analyze and understand things, but the feelings you have usually determine whether you take action— and what action you take. As discussed earlier, emotions are survival assets. They move you toward life-enhancing people or things and away from life-threatening people or things. For example, when you love or admire someone (life-enhancing), you want to be near them, and when you fear or dislike someone (life-threatening), you want to move away from them. The intensity of the emotion determines how urgently you want to act. When you are just annoyed, you may be able to ignore someone you dislike, but when you are enraged, it is much harder not to yell at the person or storm out of the room.

Emotion Myths and Truths

Myth: Some emotions are "good," and others are "bad."
Truth: All emotions inform you about what is going on in your life. An emotion may not feel good, but it is always telling you something. You just need to pay attention and find out what the message is.

Myth: You can't control your emotions.
Truth: With knowledge and practice, you can learn to manage and cope with your emotions.

Myth: You must follow your emotions.
Truth: It's important to acknowledge your emotions, but they don't have to determine what you do. You have more control over how you react to your emotions or what you choose to do than you may think.

Myth: You must ignore your emotions to make good decisions.
Truth: Emotions can provide helpful information; you need to decide how and if you will use this information in your decision-making.

> No matter how an emotion feels to you, it is important and meaningful. It is valuable data that you can transform into knowledge, which you can then use to be the best version of yourself.

By reading this chapter, I hope you've become more familiar and comfortable with the topic of emotions so you can be open to your own emotional experiences—even the yucky, difficult, stressful ones. No matter how an emotion feels to you, it is important and meaningful. It is valuable data that you can transform into knowledge, which you can then use to be the best version of yourself. The next chapter illustrates how you can accomplish this by listening with care to your feelings and discovering the meaning in the emotion.

Thinking About Feeling

The emotion chain reaction can help you identify how an emotion happens to you. Think of an emotion that you felt recently. What was the trigger that set off your emotional reaction? Was the trigger an internal or external event? How did you interpret this event—what did it mean to you? What body sensations, thoughts, or actions happened next?

CHAPTER 3

The Message in the Emotion

Emotions are messengers. Whether pleasant or unpleasant, emotions carry information. You can use this information to make decisions and set and achieve your goals.

However, emotions can be complicated and confusing sometimes. Understanding them in yourself and reading them in others are skills that take practice to develop. In this chapter you'll learn three questions that will help you improve your emotional understanding. With time, effort, and feedback, your skills will get stronger.

The Fire Alarm and the Fire

Here is a metaphor to help you understand how emotions can carry important messages. Let's consider the relationship between a fire alarm and a fire. The role of a fire alarm is to send a clear signal that a fire might be burning in the building and that everyone inside the building is in danger. The fire alarm is the messenger, and the fire is the message. A fire alarm conveys its message with loud sounds and sometimes bright lights too. The sounds and lights are hard to ignore. They get your attention and force you to focus and take action (get out).

Just as a fire alarm gets your attention to deliver information about a fire, an emotion gets your attention to convey information about yourself and other people. Let's use anxiety as an example. When you feel anxious, your racing heart, the butterflies in your stomach, your sweaty palms, and your cata-strophic thoughts get your attention to deliver the message that you are unsure about a situation that may lead to emotional or physical harm.

> ## It is critical not to focus so tightly on the experience of an emotion that you can't see what the emotion is telling you.

It is critical not to focus so tightly on the experience of an emotion that you can't see what the emotion is telling you. This would be like getting so caught up in a fire alarm (covering your ears and closing your eyes) that you ignore the alarm's message (there's a fire!) and you don't leave the building. In fact, focusing on an emotional experience instead of the emotion's message is common, especially with unpleasant or complex emotions. People may concentrate on controlling or getting rid of a "bad" feeling as soon as possible, and as a result, they do not think about the information the emotion carries.

TREY'S STORY

Trey always feels weird when their good friend Kayla talks about her new boyfriend, Eric. Every time Kayla talks about Eric, Trey's head gets hot. They feel irritated and lose track of what Kayla is saying, make a sarcastic comment, or try to change the topic. What are Trey's feelings trying to tell them?

● ● ● ●

Trey is feeling jealous, but they are struggling to acknowledge and manage such an uncomfortable emotion. Instead, they are trying to control it through distraction and sarcasm. What if Trey could identify their jealousy and try to understand it? Could Trey benefit from acknowledging that they are worried about losing their relationship with Kayla? Perhaps Trey could address this worry in a healthier way by telling Kayla about it.

Distinguishing between the messenger (fire alarm) and message (fire) aspects of an emotion is easy in a simple situation. But it can be tricky if the situation is complicated. Here are a couple of examples.

First, let's say that you are walking past a fenced-in yard. A big dog runs up to the fence and barks and growls at you. Without thinking, you may jerk away from the fence, your heart may beat quickly, and you may raise your arms in defense. In this example, it is easy to determine that you are experiencing the emotion of fear (the messenger) because you are concerned that the dog might attack or bite you (the message).

Now let's say you are applying for a selective arts program. Even though you feel enthusiastic about the program, you are procrastinating at completing the application. If someone asked if you were still interested, you would say yes, but you can't find the energy and focus to finish the forms. This doesn't make sense! How can you wish for something but then sabotage your own progress toward your goal? What are your feelings and behaviors telling you? This example is a bit trickier. In the next section, you will learn some questions you can ask yourself to help you understand your feelings in any situation.

Three Questions to Understand Your Emotions

To better understand the messages in your emotions, you can ask yourself three questions. I use this approach often to help teens make sense of their emotions and then use this understanding to make good decisions in their lives.

Question 1: What Are You Feeling?

The first step toward emotional understanding is being able to notice and name an emotion when you're experiencing it. Often this is easy, especially when you feel your emotions physically—such as by a change in your heart rate, sweating, an urge to run, or difficulty concentrating—and it's obvious your feelings have changed in this situation. But sometimes emotions can be subtle, quiet experiences, especially when there is no obvious trigger or you aren't paying attention to yourself. Have you ever had someone ask you what's wrong and only then you realized you were experiencing an emotion? Your tone of voice, facial expression, or body language revealed the emotion to others before you noticed it yourself. You might not have noticed if no one had said anything.

A simple practice that can help with noticing emotions is to check in with your body and brain every now and again. Take a few seconds to scan your body and thoughts to see what's happening. Try to pick up on changes in your body and mind that suggest you may be processing an emotion. Ask yourself, "What am I feeling right now?" This practice is called mindfulness. Don't be surprised if you notice more than one emotion. People often experience several feelings simultaneously, and each could be carrying an important message.

Once you notice an emotion, you must name it. Giving it an appropriate label is important because naming something helps you understand it better. When you label something correctly, you can make accurate predictions. For example, if you see a roundish, reddish object, you could call it an apple or a ball. If you call it an apple, then you would expect to be able to eat it and find seeds in its core. If you call the object a ball, then you would not expect to eat it and find seeds; rather, you'd expect it to bounce if you threw it against the floor. Accurate labeling and predictions can help you make good decisions.

> Accurate labeling and predictions can help you make good decisions.

Naming an emotion can be tricky because so many emotions exist, with a wide range of names. You also need to consider the intensity of your emotion. For example, you may know that a feeling you're experiencing falls into the general category of anger, but how angry are you? Do you feel displeased, upset, or enraged? It can be hard to tell. Hopefully, most emotions you experience will be familiar enough that you can easily name them. If you struggle to name your emotions, you may need to increase your emotional vocabulary. This book can help you do just that!

If you feel an emotion that's difficult to label, look for a trigger. All emotions are triggered by some external or internal event. If you can identify the trigger, it can help you label the feeling. Let's say you meet someone new when you are at the skate park. They seem nice and friendly, so you exchange contact information with them. The next day, you get a text from them asking you to meet after school at the park near their house. When you read this text, you begin to feel uncomfortable. You're not sure exactly what you're feeling, but you do know that the text message is triggering it. To get a sense of your emotion, you can ask yourself, "What about this message is making me feel uncomfortable?" This question may lead you to realize that you have never met a new acquaintance alone in a park before. Your uncertainty about doing this for the first time is triggering your discomfort. As you will read more about in chapter 7, uncertainty is usually associated with anxiety. Aha! That must be it. What you are feeling is anxiety. Now that you've noticed and named your feeling, you need to extract the message from the emotion.

Question 2: What Is This Feeling Telling You?

Emotions are data. When you experience an emotion, ask yourself what information the feeling is giving you. Emotions can tell you about yourself, your world, and others. Sometimes the message is clear. Other times you may have to work to figure it out. One way to find the message in an emotion is to consider where it is focusing your attention. Are you spending a lot of time thinking about being close to someone? Then the message might be that you're falling in love. Or are you imagining screaming at someone and telling them off? Then the message is likely anger.

Another approach to uncovering the message in the emotion is to consider how your body is feeling or acting. Are you gritting your teeth or clenching your fists? Then the message might be frustration. Or are you smiling and wanting to clap your hands? Sounds like excitement.

Sometimes emotional experiences are confusing, and you may interpret them wrong. Let's consider the example of jealousy. Jealousy is thinking that someone wants what you have and is plotting to take it away from you. You can be jealous that someone will take your possessions, your friends, or your social status. If you feel jealousy, your suspicions about someone could be right—but you might also be wrong or overreacting. How can you tell?

You can challenge your feeling of jealousy when it shows up, instead of just accepting it. For example, you may feel jealous that the new player on your team wants to take your position as captain. In response to this emotion, you could either believe your emotion as fact or you could ask yourself, "Is there evidence for my suspicion, or am I just nervous because the new player is really good?" By considering the evidence for or against your thoughts and feelings, you give yourself the opportunity to respond in a healthy and effective manner.

> By considering the evidence for or against your thoughts and feelings, you give yourself the opportunity to respond in a healthy and effective manner.

Another way to analyze emotional information is not to focus on whether the information is true or false by considering the evidence, but rather to determine if it is helpful or unhelpful in terms of moving you toward your goals. In other words, think about what you want from a situation. What is your objective? Is your emotion helping you get there? If so, go with it. If not, let go of it.

ANGELA'S STORY

Angela was new to her school. She and her family had moved from another state for her mother's new job. She had not wanted to leave her old town, because she knew a lot of people there and really enjoyed being with her friends. Now she had to start all over. The new school was in a community much wealthier than her old one. Angela noticed that some of her classmates drove cars to school instead of taking the bus as she did. They all seemed to wear the latest fashions and had the newest phones. As she sat in class on that first day, she wondered how she would ever fit in. She knew she wanted to connect with her new classmates, but maybe she was too different from them to make it work.

❦ ❦ ❦ ❦

Angela was in a situation that's common for young people who move. She was probably at least a little excited about her mom's new job and her own new opportunities, but it also meant leaving behind a life that was familiar and adapting to a new environment. Angela knew she wanted to make new friends but didn't know if she would succeed. She had a mix of feelings, but two that stand out are curiosity and anxiety. Curiosity gave her energy and the desire to reach out, but anxiety made her unsure if her new peers would like and accept her. In this situation, Angela could ask herself which of these feelings is most helpful in achieving her goal of new friendships. Curiosity is a strong motivator to engage with others. It isn't easy, and she may experience some setbacks (and anxiety). But to reach her goal, Angela must trust her social skills and give it a shot.

Question 3: What Can You Do with This Feeling?

All emotions have *action tendencies*. These are a specific set of actions that an emotion makes you want to do. You can sort emotional action tendencies into "approach" behaviors and "withdraw" behaviors. For example, fear makes you want to withdraw, or move away from, a scary object. Love, on the other hand, makes you want to approach, or move toward, the object of your affection. Many action tendencies are instinctive. They can be so strong and automatic that you may feel you have no ability to stop or manage them. This is a good thing when emotions are alerting you about danger, because a quick response can keep you safe. Emotions evolved to help humans survive and thrive, so sometimes you have to act before you think.

Despite your instinctive reactions, you do have quite a bit of say in how you respond to emotions. In fact, maturing emotionally is about developing the ability to respond to your feelings. A lot of this development occurs during adolescence.

> ### People love good feelings and would do anything to have more of them; people hate bad feelings and would do anything to have fewer of them.

But maturation isn't a smooth, straight road. Along the way you might make choices that are not healthy for you, despite your best effort. When it comes to figuring out what to do with "bad" feelings, humans have developed all kinds of unhealthy strategies. People love good feelings and would do anything to have more of them; people hate bad feelings and would do anything to have fewer of them. So when you have unpleasant, unwanted feelings, you might immediately try to avoid, change, or get rid of them. Even though this is natural, it's problematic, because emotions, whether pleasant or unpleasant, provide useful data. What important information are you sacrificing when you chase away or ignore these feelings?

In addition, many mental health conditions are exacerbated by attempts to avoid or control unpleasant feelings. The more you try to get rid of feelings instead of listening to them, the more troublesome the emotions become. For example, individuals with a condition called social anxiety disorder try to limit their exposure to distressing feelings of anxiety and rejection by avoiding social situations. However, the more successful they are at avoiding people, the more anxious and alone they feel over time, and the more problematic their condition becomes.

Russ Harris, a medical doctor who treats emotional problems, often says in his books and articles that control is not the solution; it's the problem. By this he means that emotions are not controllable, but many people try to do it anyway—and that causes problems. Dr. Harris uses the acronym *DOTS* to describe the strategies people use to control (avoid or get rid of) their emotions:

- **Distraction:** Distraction is engaging in behaviors that take your mind off painful thoughts and feelings. For example, you might mindlessly watch movies or shows, play video games, scroll on your phone, exercise, or obsessively study for an exam. Have you ever had a school project to do but you really, *really* did not want to do it? Maybe it bored, annoyed, or worried you. To avoid these feelings, maybe you decided to play video games "just to relax for a bit," only to look up several hours later and realize that it was bedtime and you now had to stay up all night to get the project done.

- **Opting out:** Opting out is staying away from or withdrawing from important, meaningful, or life-enhancing activities, events, tasks, challenges, or people because they might make you feel "bad." You might be opting out if you ignore an important phone call or text because the caller may ask you a difficult or uncomfortable question.

- **Thinking:** Have you ever found yourself trying to think your way out of a problem? This strategy is unhelpful when your mind gets stuck in an endless loop, such as worrying about the future or continuously rehashing a past failure. Thorough and diligent thinking is important for problem-solving, but sometimes you might get stuck on the "hamster wheel" of your mind instead of making changes where it really matters: in your real-world life.

- **Substances and other strategies:** Some teens may try to control their uncomfortable emotions by using substances and behaviors to try to feel better. Substances might include drugs, alcohol, or cigarettes. Behaviors might include unsafe sexual activity; sleeping; shopping; undereating or overeating; self-harming by cutting, scratching, or burning; or even attempting suicide. These attempts to get rid of bad feelings ultimately cause more trouble, even if they offer a few moments of relief.

As you read the last section, you may have been surprised by some of the activities described as unhealthy ways to deal with bad feelings. After all, aren't sleep, exercising, studying for exams, and avoiding stressful situations ways that you can stay healthy and increase your success? The answer depends on whether you are using these strategies to avoid bad feelings. For example, shopping can be a necessary, fun, or rewarding adventure if you have the money, need the items, or use it as a means for socializing. But what happens when shopping becomes your go-to way of dealing with unwanted feelings? Would that mean every time you have an unpleasant feeling, you would have to buy something? What impact would that have on your budget?

Any attempt to avoid, control, or get rid of unwanted feelings could make the situation worse. So what can you do with your feelings instead? Well, the same thing you would do with any valuable information: use it to make your life better! The rest of this book is dedicated to helping you understand the message in some of the emotions you will experience as a teenager and to giving you a range of ways you can use emotions to your benefit.

Thinking About Feeling

Every emotion carries a message. Paying attention to the message can help you relate to others, make decisions, and achieve your goals. Think of a pleasant feeling you've had recently. What is the name of that emotion? What does it tell you about yourself, your life, and your relationships? Name one way you could use this information to improve your life.

CHAPTER 4
Love

JASON'S STORY

Jason had taken only slight notice of Britney before Mr. Benson assigned them to be partners on the midyear precalculus project. He had always thought Britney was nice, but he never really thought of her as his type. Some of his friends thought she was kind of cute, but he always saw himself with someone more outgoing. Britney was quiet, and she was more interested in anime than sports and parties.

The project turned out to be challenging. Jason and Britney had to spend many evenings together working hard at it. The more they worked and talked, the more Jason realized that he really enjoyed being with Britney. He discovered that she was more than nice; she was also smart, kind, and hilarious. And her eyes . . . why hadn't he noticed them before? He found himself thinking about her often, and his heart beat a little faster every time she was around. He was slowly starting to see that there was something special about Britney.

Ah . . . love. What a wonderful, confusing feeling. What is love, anyway? Why does it overwhelm you, causing you to be fully and completely absorbed and focused on a specific person or thing?

If you are confused about love, you are in good company. The scientific community can't figure it out either. Scientists disagree on whether love is even an emotion. Some argue that it is not an emotion because it does not cause easily observable physical reactions. Many emotions include clearly visible facial expressions and body movements. Disgust, for example, is observable in wide-open eyes, a crinkled-up nose, and sometimes a tongue sticking out. Anger is observable in clenched teeth, tight lips, and squinted or glaring eyes. What about love? What facial expression indicates that you are in love? How does your body move when you feel love for someone? It's hard to say.

People also disagree on whether the various types of love that humans experience are the same feeling. There is love for family, pets, and friends; love for self; and the romantic and sexual love you can feel for a partner. There is even love for abstract concepts such as art, music, food, and places, such as one's hometown or country. People use the word *love* to express a wide range of human interactions with others and the world. These experiences are unique combinations of body sensations, thoughts, and actions.

Perhaps love is not an emotion at all, but a drive, more like thirst or hunger. Drives are urges to satisfy basic human needs. Some scientists argue that love helps people satisfy the fundamental human need of closeness to others and sets the stage for sexual reproduction. I question this view of love, because drives go away when the needs are met. For example, when you drink water, you are no longer thirsty. However, love tends to stay strong even after you have formed a connection with your love interest.

Here's another perspective: love may not be just one emotion, but several simultaneous emotions. This view is based on the idea that primary emotions can combine to create more complex emotions. For example, some people describe depression as a blend of sadness and anger. Love may be a combination of joy, excitement, anxiety, and who knows what else!

Whether love is one emotion or a combination of emotions, I consider it some sort of emotion. Chapter 3 describes how emotions are messengers. They inform you about yourself, others, and the world, helping you focus your resources, communicate, and move to action. This is exactly what love does. It informs you that you value someone or something. It inspires you to focus your resources and take action to create and maintain a connection with the valued person or thing.

> Love informs you that you value someone or something. It inspires you to focus your resources and take action to create and maintain a connection with the valued person or thing.

However you label love, it is a powerful feeling that you will likely experience during your teenage years. A better understanding of it will, hopefully, help you feel less overwhelmed when that happens.

The Experience of Love

Body Sensations

No pattern of clearly visible facial expressions and body movements is associated with love. But if you look beyond observable physical reactions, you'll find an array of important changes in the brain and body.

When you experience love for someone, your brain produces hormones that make you feel pleasure and stress at the same time, and these hormones can cause changes in the body. Some of these hormones make you feel "warm and fuzzy" (happy and content) and at the same time aggressive and territorial. You might feel warmth when you think about your sweetheart and competitive when potential rivals are around. These hormones may also lead to physical reactions, such as sweaty palms, increased heart rate, and butterflies in your stomach. When you are in the presence of your loved one, looking at them may make your pupils dilate, and you often can't help but smile and laugh.

When you feel love, activity in the part of your brain associated with fear decreases. Fear warns you to make good judgments and follow rules. Decreased activity in this area may explain the questionable choices people may make when they are in love. For example, even if you always obey your curfew, you may consider staying out late to be with your love interest.

Thoughts

When you're feeling love, the impact of love on your thinking is typically quite simple: all you can do is think about your love interest. You think about being with them, and when you are apart, you think about what they are doing, you worry about them, and you miss them. Sometimes your thoughts may be intrusive and continuous, and you may have trouble concentrating on anything else. When the object of your love is not a person but a thing, concept, or experience, the impact on your thoughts is similar. If you've found yourself spending a lot of time thinking about an activity or a place, it is safe to say you love it!

Actions

Like your thoughts, your actions when you are in love have one purpose: to bring you closer to the person you love. You may be feeling both stress and pleasure, and depending on the situation and the factors at play, you may find yourself motivated more by one than by the other. For example, if you are overwhelmed by the stress, you may be weak in the knees and unable to speak, or perhaps focused on your jealousy and a sense of not deserving your love interest. On the other hand, if your pleasure response is strong, you may be willing to do almost anything to be close to your beloved, including actions that are out of character, or unlike your usual behavior. Love is a powerful emotion, and it can reveal aspects of people that they themselves never knew existed.

Love is a powerful emotion, and it can reveal aspects of people that they themselves never knew existed.

Love Myths and Truths

Myth: There is no such thing as love at first sight.
Truth: It depends on how you define the word *love*. An initial attraction to someone is hardly the long-term closeness and partnership that people usually think about when they hear the word *love*. One way you can think of an immediate attraction is as a crush. A crush is a strong romantic infatuation with someone. When you have a crush on someone, you see them as really attractive or special in some way—their looks, personality, style, or achievements. You want to know and hang out with them, but you may also feel anxious about whether they will like you. As you get older, immediate attraction to someone may be more about lust, or a desire to be physically close or sexually intimate with them.

Myth: Opposites attract.
Truth: When it comes to relationships, a more accurate saying is *birds of a feather flock together*. Romantic partners are often more similar than different. They may differ in superficial ways, but people tend to pick partners who share their values, religion,

education, and interests. Imagine you meet someone for the first time and are attracted to them. You start to talk, and the first few statements they make about their interests, hobbies, beliefs, and values are completely opposite of yours. Are you likely to ask them out? Maybe, but you are less likely to develop a relationship with them.

Living with Love

If you are experiencing love for the first time, it can be confusing and overwhelming. Is there any experience that produces more pleasure and misery, often at the same time, than falling in love? It can be challenging to sort out your feelings and form a love partnership with another person.

Is there any experience that produces more pleasure and misery, often at the same time, than falling in love?

Anthropologist Helen Fisher has studied the experience of falling in love and proposes a helpful way of thinking about the process. She argues that falling in love occurs in three stages. In each stage, different things happen in the brain. Perhaps by becoming familiar with these stages, you can make better sense of your love experiences.

The first stage of love is lust, or physical attraction. This is "love at first sight." This is the stage in which you are consumed by the idea of being with your love interest physically. When you think about getting to know the person, it is mainly to get close to them—literally. Fisher argues that lust is about physical gratification. During this stage, you are not primarily interested in the object of your attraction as a long-term partner.

The second stage of love is romantic attraction. In this stage, individuals find themselves thinking about and obsessing about their love interest. It's no longer just about physical intimacy; you are "in love" and want to be interacting with your partner constantly. During this stage, you may find that you are less hungry and less sleepy. You might even forgo food and sleep just to stay on the phone with your love interest.

The third stage of love is attachment. This stage can last many years. During the attachment stage, your brain releases chemicals, such as oxytocin, which promote bonding behaviors. Dr. Fisher argues that this stage of love is necessary for humans to build families together. (Although it's not the only requirement, of course.) As any parent will tell you, raising kids is not only rewarding but also challenging. Feelings of attachment provide some of the stability, responsibility, and commitment necessary to meet the challenges of maintaining a family and raising children.

So what does all this mean for a teenager in love? It means you can blame your confused feelings and thoughts on your brain! If not for your brain releasing all those wild hormones when you see someone you like, falling in love might be much simpler. As bewildered as love may make you feel, it is normal. As strange as you may feel at times when you are experiencing love, it is all a natural part of being human. (For more information on understanding when love becomes heartbreak, see chapter 6 on sadness.)

Thinking About Feeling

You might experience love in relation
to a specific activity. This could be any
activity you really enjoy, such as playing a sport, making art, singing, acting,
coding, or participating in role-playing
games. Engaging in your beloved activity regularly can help you de-stress
and improve your self-confidence. What
activity do you love? What, if any, other
emotions describe how you feel when you
participate in this activity?

CHAPTER 5
Anger

GRACE'S STORY

"But you said I could go to the party!" Grace screamed at her mother.

Her mother glared back at her. "Grace, I made it clear that you could go to Lawanda's party if you improved your grade in math this cycle. So tell me, did you improve that grade?"

Grace knew her mother had a point. She'd put more effort into her studies this cycle, but she'd slacked off at the end and did poorly on her exam. This had dropped her grade back to a C, just like last semester.

But she had tried! Why couldn't her mother see this and let her go to the party? Grace was infuriated. Her heart raced and tears welled in her eyes. She couldn't even think clearly.

* * * *

Scientists generally agree that anger is a basic human emotion. All people are born with the capacity to get angry, and all experience anger sometimes. Even babies get angry! Have you ever seen a toddler rolling around on the floor screaming and crying? That's pure anger, expressed freely.

You experience anger when you perceive that someone has purposely or neglectfully done you wrong or caused you emotional or physical pain. Anger can keep you safe and minimize threats. Anger protects you by urging you to act against the person, situation, or thing that triggered your anger. You might act verbally, physically, or by having thoughts of aggression—or all of these at once. Imagine that someone calls you an idiot in front of all your other friends. You would likely see this as an attack against you, and it would probably trigger anger. You might feel a desire to get back at the person who insulted you. You may feel an urge to insult them back or even confront them physically.

Anger not only protects you from the behaviors of others, it also protects you from uncomfortable feelings. It is sometimes called the "substitute emotion" or the "cover-up emotion" because it often shows up after you experience another uncomfortable emotion. Let's say a friend playfully trips you, and you stumble. You might first feel a flash of embarrassment. But anger may follow immediately. The anger substitutes for or covers up the more unpleasant feeling of embarrassment. This emotion replacement process happens unconsciously. It occurs mainly with painful, self-diminishing feelings, such as guilt, shame, rejection, sadness, loneliness, disappointment, fear, or frustration. These feelings make you feel weak, vulnerable, and passive, but anger is a powerful and active emotion. It fills you with energy and moves you to act against the source of the threat. Although anger is a difficult feeling, people tend to find it more bearable than self-diminishing feelings.

Anger shifts your attention away from your own suffering.

Anger shifts your attention away from your own suffering. This emotion substitution strategy is common in humans. In fact, in many cultures around the world, it is more acceptable to display anger than to show vulnerable emotions. Of course, emotion substitution is all an illusion. The shame or disappointment or other emotion is still there, simmering under the anger. Try as you might to fool yourself, in the end you still must find a way to deal with your underlying feeling of weakness and vulnerability.

Think about the last time you experienced intense anger. Then dig deeper into your feelings. What else do you find? Buried under the anger, you may well discover a more difficult emotion. Are you dealing with that other feeling, or are you tricking yourself by focusing on your anger?

Let's look at how anger plays out by considering the body sensations, thoughts, and actions associated with the emotion.

The Experience of Anger

Body Sensations

When you are angry, your body immediately goes into defense mode. It releases the hormone adrenaline, which gives you a rush of energy, tightens your muscles, increases your heart rate, and raises your blood pressure. These physical changes get your body prepared to react—or more specifically, to attack.

Thoughts

When you are angry, your first thought may be to get rid of the source of your anger—whether it's a person, situation, or thing—in an aggressive way. Your attention becomes tightly focused on what is causing you to feel threatened. Your mind may scan the list of options for removing the threat. The intensity of your anger depends on how you assess the threat. You're probably more angry when you think the threat is intentional. You're probably less angry when you think the threat is accidental or due to carelessness. Or you may be more angry when your suffering is severe, and less angry when the suffering is mild. For example, have you ever stubbed your toe on a rock and gotten angry at the rock? Of course you know the rock did not mean to get in your way. But you still might get really angry at it because your toe is throbbing with pain!

> Have you ever stubbed your toe on a rock and gotten angry at the rock? Of course you know the rock did not mean to get in your way. But you still might get really angry at it because your toe is throbbing with pain!

Actions

Angry actions vary depending on the cause of anger, the situation, and the available resources. The goal of angry acts is to vigorously remove the source of the threat. Angry actions fall into two main categories: destructive and constructive.

Destructive angry acts are often impulsive. When you act in this way, you do not consider the impact on others or yourself. You are trying aggressively to get rid of the threat. For example, if you get angry at someone and proceed to swear at them and beat them up, you may experience serious consequences. You might get in trouble with parents, teachers, or even the law. You could develop a negative reputation with others. You could suffer physical harm while fighting.

Constructive angry behaviors, on the other hand, are focused on resolving conflict in a nonviolent way. If you take this approach, you are saying that you have been wronged, but you believe you might be able to resolve the situation by engaging with the offender and telling them what you need. For example, you could speak up firmly and tell them you don't appreciate their behavior and ask them to stop. You might also reach out to others who could help you resolve the conflict, such as a teacher, parent, or other authority figure. A constructive approach is assertive, but not aggressive. It requires more self-control, which might be challenging, but it can also bring better, safer, longer-lasting results for everyone.

Anger Myths and Truths

Myth: Anger is bad.
Truth: It is not helpful to think about anger, or any emotion, as good or bad. Even if an emotion feels unpleasant, as anger often can, it is more about whether you express it in constructive or destructive ways. Anger is about self-protection. It can help you stand up for yourself and for people or things that are important to you. It can help you focus your energy on defending yourself and others from harm.

Myth: Your anger controls you.
Truth: Anger does mobilize your body and mind. It marshals all your systems to defend you. This may leave you feeling controlled by your anger. But you don't *have* to behave aggressively or destructively. You can improve how you act when you are angry by learning and practicing healthy anger management and conflict resolution skills. You can use your body and mind to manage your anger. For example, taking deep breaths can be an effective strategy for keeping anger positive. It can also be helpful to stop and think about the consequences of acting aggressively toward someone. You may feel justified, but when you take a little time to think it through, you realize rash actions may get you kicked off a team or sent to the principal's office. You may also suffer a negative social consequence, such as getting a reputation for having a short fuse or being out of control. Or your reckless behavior may be recorded by a bystander and posted on social media. When you realize you are angry, you can choose to make safer and healthier decisions about how to behave.

Living with Anger

Like all other emotions, anger carries messages about your-self, others, and the world—specifically, about whether you are under threat. It is important to have such an alert system, because it helps you avoid physical and emotional damage. But anger is a challenge when your alert system keeps giving false alarms or won't shut off. You may find yourself responding with anger when the threat is minimal or nonexistent. For example, if a friend playfully scolds you, you may overreact and respond as if they are out to hurt you. If you can't turn down your anger and listen, you may continue to be mad even when a threat is gone—or when you realize it wasn't really a threat. Past experience is a big factor in such situations. Perhaps a present incident reminds you of a similar incident of unfairness, injustice, or pain in the past, and you respond as if it were the same situation. In these circumstances, you can benefit from having clear and effective strategies to use, such as deep breathing, relaxation, and visualization.

Deep Breathing

If you pay attention to how you breathe when you are angry, you'll notice your breaths are quick and shallow. This is a typical anger reaction; it is a fight-flight-or-freeze bodily response. Your brain notices this body reaction and reads it as evidence that you are, in fact, under threat.

Deep breathing helps you send your brain a different signal. By breathing deeply, which is something people usually do when they feel calm and safe, you tell your brain that there's nothing to worry about. Your brain then tells your body to return to a state of calm.

One helpful way to use this strategy is to pick any number between one and ten and take that many deep breaths when you feel angry. If you don't feel better after those breaths, you can do another round. Breathing is something you have to do anyway, so it's nice to know that you can use an easy breathing technique to help you feel better and behave in a safe manner.

Visualization

When you get angry, your thoughts and mental images may focus on what you can do to harm, to get back at, or to get away from the person, situation, or thing threatening you. As long as these thoughts fill your brain, you will continue to experience anger. To break this cycle, you can choose to sit, close your eyes, and bring new thoughts to mind that are associated with other feelings. For example, instead of thinking about punching someone who angered you, you could imagine a beach scene with crashing waves and a vibrant sunset. It's hard to feel angry when you're relaxing at the beach! By imagining a relaxing scene, you can distract yourself from anger and encourage your mind toward a more pleasant or helpful emotion.

Relaxation

Relaxation means to engage in behaviors that release tension from your body. For example, if you're angry, instead of tensing your muscles and getting ready for combat, you can engage in a process of tightening and then relaxing various parts of your body sequentially. Repeating this process with your feet, legs, abdomen, hands, arms, shoulders, neck, and face can help you calm your body and mind. This technique is even more effective when combined with deep breathing and visualization.

Thinking About Feeling

Anger can lead to growth when it inspires you to work at addressing injustice. Think about an issue affecting your local community or larger society that angers you. How can you use this feeling to make a positive change in your community or the world?

CHAPTER 6
Sadness

Amal heard a knock on her bedroom door. It was her dad. He was leaving today.

After four years of constant arguing, her parents were breaking up. Amal still could not believe it. Her parents' conflict bothered her, but she'd always held onto hope that they would work things out. They hadn't. About a month ago, her parents had called her to a meeting in the living room and told her that they had decided to divorce. Amal remembered crying that whole night. She could not get past the feeling of emptiness and sadness.

Her dad knocked again. "Come in, Dad," Amal said shakily. She could feel the tears welling up in her eyes.

* * * *

The root of sadness is loss—the loss of things and especially the loss of people. When you feel the powerful pull of sadness, your body is telling you that something or someone you wish to be close to is no longer available to you. You may have memories and constant reminders, but you no longer have access to the person or thing. Sadness can make you feel empty and hollow.

You might also feel sadness when you realize that you will not get something you want. This could be a relationship with a love interest, a grade, a job, an opportunity, attention from others, or even new clothing. Sometimes the loss of an abstract concept can trigger sadness too. For example, you might feel sad if you lose your health through injury or illness or if you lose faith, power, hope, or trust.

Sadness can be painful and overwhelming, but it can also be beneficial. Sadness centers you and helps you understand when something or someone is important to you. You reflect on the value of the person or thing in your life, and you feel the impact deeply.

> ## Sadness centers you and helps you understand when something or someone is important to you.

Although sadness is important, informative, and normal, humans work hard to not experience this pain. People often lie to themselves, fake being happy, or use substances, such as alcohol or drugs, to try to numb their sad feelings. They may fear that if they allow themselves to feel sad, the sadness will grow and overwhelm them. In fact, the opposite happens. When you allow yourself to experience your sad feelings, not only does the pain ultimately subside, but you may come out the other side of it feeling calmer, stronger, and clearer about yourself and others.

The Experience of Sadness

Body Sensations

When you're sad, your body seems to want to slow down or shut down. You have little energy and may have difficulty concentrating. You may experience an ache or sense of emptiness in your stomach. You might cry. Some scientists say crying sends a message to others that you need attention and support. Crying also releases stress hormones from the body. Finally, when you are sad, you may experience changes in your appetite and sleep; they might increase, decrease, or become irregular.

Crying sends a message to others that you need attention and support.

Thoughts

Sadness can make it hard to concentrate on anything other than your loss. You may begin to ruminate, or think repeatedly, about your past connection to the lost person, thing, or concept. Even when you try to put it out of your mind, the thoughts may keep returning. You might fantasize about what it would be like if you hadn't lost the person, thing, or concept.

Actions

You may feel tired and lack energy when you're sad. You might have little motivation to do anything except reflect on what you've lost and maybe cry. You may want to be alone or to interact only with others who understand your situation. You might avoid other people—even your friends—because you don't want them to see that you're sad. You might feel ashamed or embarrassed to show your sadness to others.

Sadness Myths and Truths

Myth: Sadness is the same as depression.
Truth: This is a common misconception. The feelings are related, but they are not the same. Sadness tends to focus on a specific loss or difficult situation, whereas depression is feeling

that you'll never be happy, safe, loved, or successful again. (It may stem from a loss or difficult situation, but not necessarily.) In other words: depression is a more intense, chronic, and debilitating form of sadness, perhaps with a side of anger, shame, and guilt. It casts a dark cloud over everything. For example, if you are sad that your hockey team lost a key game, you might not enjoy going to practice for a few days. But if you become depressed, you not only don't enjoy practice, you also feel down about other aspects of your life, such as school, friendships, and other activities.

As bad as depression may feel, it is still a normal human emotion in that it generally lasts only a few days. Clinical depression is more severe, more complex, and lasts a lot longer. I differentiate them as "small d" for ordinary depression and "big D" for clinical depression. Clinical depression, or major depressive disorder (MDD), is a mental illness diagnosed when a person meets certain cognitive and behavioral criteria. Clinical depression is a large, noticeable decrease in someone's ability to manage day-to-day functions. It may include increased sadness, emptiness, and tiredness, as well as decreased interest or pleasure in life activities, for at least two weeks. Children and teenagers may feel irritable and have a short temper. Clinical depression also affects one's concentration, appetite or weight, sleep, and energy level. A clinically depressed person likely has strong feelings of worthlessness and may have thoughts of death and suicide. They may feel that they have no ability to make changes in their world and that they are doomed to despair.

Myth: Crying is weakness.
Truth: No clear scientific evidence connects tears with weakness. Crying is simply a human expression of emotion whose meaning varies among cultures. It is a natural response to a strong emotion. All humans cry, at least until their preteens. This shift may be because of social pressure. Some cultures

consider crying a weakness because it is a behavior common in children, who cry easily and often. So, when an adult or teen cries, it may suggest to some that the person is easily overwhelmed or not in control of their emotions. Tears can indeed be uncontrollable, and the floodgates can open unexpectedly.

At the same time, crying is an important source of emotional communication. It tells others that you are in pain and need solace and support. Sadness is most recognizable when accompanied by tears. A sad face without tears can be confused with other feelings, leading onlookers to be unsure about giving aid. Tears can also have a self-soothing effect, both physically and emotionally. Have you heard of "having a good cry"? Crying may be healing, especially when you are alone or around people who are understanding and supportive.

Living with Sadness

The most important thing to remember about sadness is that it is a normal human emotion. It happens to everyone sometimes, and it may be a necessary feeling to help you explore and understand your connections to people and things that you have lost. Usually you won't need any specialized skills or techniques to deal with sadness, because it tends to resolve quickly on its own. Sadness feels powerful while it is happening, but it generally weakens with time.

When you feel sad, you can help your process along by facing it directly and not trying to avoid or ignore it. For example, if you're missing somebody, you could focus on positive memories of them instead of the negative impact their loss has had on you. You could do this through simple rituals, such as calling or writing a person who has moved, looking through albums or visiting the grave of someone who has died, or by connecting with other people who also miss the person. These rituals give you the opportunity to cope with your sadness in a structured and supportive way.

For many teens, one of the most intense experiences of sadness happens after the loss of a romantic relationship or rejection from a potential relationship. Many people have their first romantic relationship or attraction during their teen years. When that relationship ends—or fails to start—the pain can be overwhelming.

If you experience this kind of loss or another relationship loss, you may want to isolate yourself, and you may find yourself thinking repeatedly about what went wrong and what you could have done better. You might judge yourself or the other person harshly. Some alone time may be helpful to think about what happened, but too much alone time could lead you to a darker place of self-loathing. As difficult as it may seem in the moment, one of the best ways to deal with this type of sadness is to seek support from close friends and family. Their comfort during this period can be helpful and healing. They may not always say the right thing, but just by listening and supporting you, they can help you move past your grief.

Thinking About Feeling

Sadness is a feeling people often struggle to talk about. They may think saying "I'm sad" to others will make them feel too vulnerable. It's more important to pay attention to the message in the emotion you are experiencing than it is to use the specific word *sadness*. Many other words describe sadness, or the feeling of loss. Can you think of five words you or your friends use instead of *sad*?

CHAPTER 7
Anxiety

KWAME'S STORY

Kwame sat at his desk in math class. It was final exam day. He had been studying every night for the past week, but he still did not feel ready. Mr. Benson was standing in front of the room holding the stack of exams. He was saying something about "do your best," but Kwame could barely hear it over his pounding heart. He grabbed his pencil and realized his palms were sweaty. He rubbed them furiously on his sweatshirt. What if he hadn't studied enough? What if his mind went blank? What if he failed math? Would he be able to graduate? He took a deep breath and looked at Mr. Benson, who'd finished his pep talk and was now handing out the exam booklets. It was game time.

◦ ◦ ◦ ◦

Anxiety is one of the most common feelings humans experience. It is an emotional reaction to uncertainty or doubt. This uncertainty or doubt tends to be about an unknown future outcome. Anxiety is a sense of apprehension or dread over a coming danger or threat. You may feel anxious when you think you're not ready, willing, or able to address a situation effectively. In other words, your knowledge, skills, and experience will not be enough to help you avoid an unpleasant or unknown outcome in that situation. Anxiety can range from normal apprehension about everyday uncertainties (Will I miss the bus? Do I have spinach in my teeth?) to intense and unbearable phobias (fear and avoidance of specific things, such as dogs, needles, or spiders) and even panic attacks. Panic attacks are when a person gets so anxious that they feel they will faint, have a stroke or a heart attack, or even die.

Anxiety is related to fear, but anxiety and fear differ in important ways. Fear tends to be aroused by specific, immediate threats of bodily or psychological harm. For example, if someone raises their hand to strike you or you hear a loud bang, you feel fear about something that's happening in that moment. Anxiety is more future-oriented. It's the anticipation that something bad or unknown will happen. It is about your *thought* that something bad or unknown is going to happen— not about anything that is *actually* happening. Anxiety is a vaguer emotion than fear. It may be focused on a particular target (person, thing, or situation), but the potential outcome of the threat is usually uncertain. You might feel fear when you see a dog running toward you with its teeth bared because it's clearly aiming to attack you. You may feel anxious when you see a dog off its leash, even if it's not doing anything threatening, because you think it *could* attack you. Fear is a reaction to a clear and present danger, while anxiety is a reaction to an unclear and potential danger.

Anxiety is sometimes called "stress," but anxiety and stress are not the same thing. They have a chicken-and-egg relationship. That means either can cause the other.

CHICKEN AND EGG

A chicken-and-egg relationship is an unsolvable puzzle. This expression comes from the saying *Which came first, the chicken or the egg*? There's no logical answer to this question. Chickens lay eggs, so did the chicken exist first? But chickens also come from eggs—so did the egg exist first?

Stress is the strain and tension you feel in negative or demanding situations. Stress itself is not inherently bad. In fact, scientists differentiate between eustress, which is "good" stress, and distress, which is "bad" stress. The terms *good* and *bad* in this context refer to your perception of the stressful situation.

You feel eustress when you face a challenge that you perceive as within or only slightly beyond your ability to handle. You see this challenge as difficult but doable and worthwhile. You believe the outcome will be successful. An example of eustress would be what a runner feels while preparing for a challenging race. It will be hard work, and possibly physically painful, but it will also be enjoyable and maybe even winnable.

The opposite of eustress is distress. You feel distress when you think you're totally incapable of dealing with a situation. You perceive that the task is too big or that you don't have the resources to deal with it. You feel overwhelmed. Your body and mind may kick into fight-flight-or-freeze mode and may trigger anxiety. Anxiety is an emotional reaction to perceived stress. When your mind perceives a situation as distressing (beyond your ability), then the outcome becomes uncertain and the task feels undoable. This uncertainty leads to feelings of anxiety.

At other times, the cause-and-effect relationship is reversed, and anxiety triggers stress instead. Imagine you have a health condition that requires you to visit the doctor often for checkups. You may have to undergo a serious surgical procedure if the checkup suggests that you need it. Would you be anxious before every checkup? You might feel that you can't handle this ongoing anxiety, and therefore you experience the whole situation as stressful. The uncertainty of your diagnosis leads to anxiety, and the constant, repeated anxiety is the negative condition that triggers stress.

The Experience of Anxiety

Body Sensations

Anxiety is your natural fight-flight-or-freeze response to a thought that something bad or unknown is going to happen. Animals, including humans, respond to danger by fighting it off, running away from it, or trying to blend into their environment. A possum, for example, will freeze in its tracks, drop to the ground, and play dead when it's frightened. Fight-flight-or-freeze responses require your body to shift energy toward preparation for intense physical activity, such as increasing the heart rate and tensing the muscles. As the energy leaves the parts of your body that aren't essential during a crisis (such as your stomach), you may feel light-headed or have butterflies in your stomach.

> Avoiding can be helpful in the short term, but it may be bad for you in the long run.

Thoughts

Anxious thoughts tend to focus on the perceived danger of the situation or your perceived ability to handle the danger. You may worry that you will be physically or emotionally harmed by the potential threat or that you won't know what to do when the threat is upon you. Like Kwame, for example, before an exam, you may panic if you start to think you didn't study enough. When you are anxious, your thoughts tend to go to the extremes. Dr. Daniel Amen, a clinical researcher and psychiatrist, coined the term ANTs (automatic negative thoughts) for these unhelpful, distorted, irrational thoughts that show up when you are anxious or experiencing other difficult emotions. Here are a few examples of ANTs:

- **Fortune-telling** is when you predict the future without a shred of evidence or data to back up your prediction. These predictions always say that something bad will happen.

- **Mind reading** is when you think you know for sure what someone else is thinking—without asking the person. And of course, they must be thinking the worst about you.

- **Blame** is an oldie but goodie! Blame is putting all the responsibility for a bad outcome on someone else.

- **All-or-nothing thinking** is when you overgeneralize or exaggerate a situation, using words like *always*, *never*, *nobody*, and so on. For example, when you feel anxious that your love interest may break up with you, you may think, "Nobody is ever going to want to be with me."

Actions

Anxiety response behaviors fall into two main categories. The first approach is about control or problem-solving. When you feel anxious, you jump into action and/or try to think through and resolve the issue. The second approach is avoidance. When you feel anxious, you stay away from the situation and try not to think about it. Avoiding can be helpful in the short term, but it may be bad for you in the long run. For example, avoiding studying for a difficult exam may help you feel better in the moment, but it will cost you in the future.

Anxiety Myths and Truths

Myth: Anxiety is a mental disorder.

Truth: Anxiety is a normal human emotion and is different from the range of mental health conditions officially classified as anxiety disorders. Conditions listed as anxiety disorders include social anxiety disorder, panic disorder, phobias, generalized anxiety disorder, and others. To know if you have one of these diagnosable anxiety conditions, you need to be assessed by a mental health clinician and meet certain criteria. Anxiety is considered disordered when it is intense, frequent, long-lasting, disproportionate to the situation, and when it significantly impacts your functioning. According to the Anxiety and Depression Association of America, this level of anxiety occurs in only about 8 percent of children and teenagers. This suggests that most people who think they have an anxiety disorder are likely dealing with the common, unpleasant, everyday type of anxiety. However, if you feel like your anxiety might be disordered, talk to an adult about making an appointment with a mental health professional.

Myth: If I eat right and exercise, I will get rid of my anxiety.

Truth: A healthy diet and exercise are important for managing stress, so it's a good idea to take care of yourself physically. But if you are human, you will never avoid or get rid of *all* anxiety, and even if you could, it wouldn't really be a good thing. As unpleasant as anxiety can be, it is a normal human reaction to stress and uncertainty. Think about how much helpful information you might lose if you never felt anxious. A better goal would be to understand and manage your anxiety, not remove it. The next section will talk more about anxiety management.

If you are human, you will never avoid or get rid of all anxiety, and even if you could, it wouldn't really be a good thing.

Living with Anxiety

Anxiety happens often. There is no question that clinical anxiety needs to be treated, but does everyday anxiety need to be eradicated? I and other scientists say no.

Anxiety can protect you from the unknown and the unfamiliar, especially when you feel that either would be harmful to you. Anxiety can help keep you safe from real-life dangers. The world can indeed be a scary place—but not all the threats you perceive are things that will actually harm you. The sometimes-scary world is where you learn new things, meet new people, and engage in new activities. It is where you grow. If you always respond to anxiety by trying to avoid it or get rid of it, you may limit your opportunities to take risks that lead to growth. If you stay focused on being safe in response to anxiety, instead of challenging yourself to take action even when you feel anxious, you may ultimately feel less safe and less happy.

So what is the lesson here? You can use the feeling of anxiety as a caution sign rather than a stop sign. When you feel anxious, try to take it as a sign to quickly reflect on your thoughts and then ask yourself what you will gain or lose by forging ahead. If there is clearly more to gain, then perhaps you need to just take a deep breath and do it. Running away from the uncertainties in life is ultimately more detrimental than taking your chances for growth.

Thinking About Feeling

To choose growth is to choose stress. What does this statement mean to you? Think of an area of your life where you are choosing stress because you've decided to take on a challenge that offers you the possibility of meaningful growth. How do you deal with the stress and anxiety you face in this situation?

CHAPTER 8

Jealousy and Envy

OSCAR'S STORY

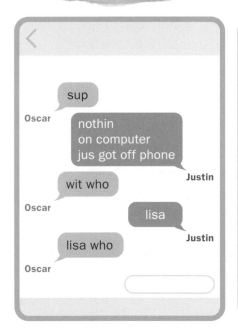

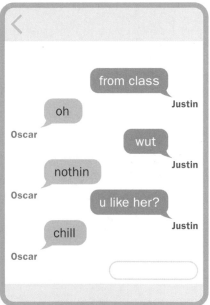

Oscar is clearly having an emotion about Justin talking to Lisa. If you had to label that emotion, what might you call it? Jealousy? Envy? Jealousy and envy are related emotions. Both are about wanting something or someone. The words *jealousy* and *envy* are often used interchangeably, but they have different meanings and perspectives. They give you different information about yourself and others. Jealousy is what you feel when someone wants what you already possess. You fear you will lose something you hold dear. Envy is what you feel when you desire what someone else has. This could be an object, a status, a relationship, an attribute, or an opportunity.

Psychologists who study the origins of emotions say that jealousy and envy both help humans survive and thrive. To prosper, people need to form and maintain interpersonal bonds—and they need to get and keep material resources. Envy helps you identify, pursue, and obtain important resources and social connections, and jealousy helps you hang on to these resources and connections by keeping you alert to potential competitors.

Jealousy and envy are also about social comparison. You may feel envy or jealousy when you compare yourself with another person. When you feel jealous, you believe you are in a superior position and that others want what you have. For example, if you believe a new classmate wants to "steal" your best friend, you feel jealous. The purpose of this emotion is to help you retain "ownership" by keeping an eye on your competition. Of course, nobody owns anybody else; your best friend is an individual human being and not your possession. But jealousy can make you feel that your friend is "yours," and that your connection is under threat.

When you feel envious, you believe you are in an inferior position because you don't have what someone else has. This difference in status causes you emotional pain. You think that if you can just get what they have, you will feel better. Let's say you are the new kid at school. You notice that one of your classmates is smart and kind and funny—and you'd like to be friends, but they are clearly close friends with another student. When you see these friends together, you feel envious. The purpose of this emotion is to focus and motivate you to get something you desire: a friendship with someone you admire.

The Experience of Jealousy

Body Sensations

Neuroscientists say that when you are jealous, the brain regions associated with fear, anger, and disgust kick into action. When these brain regions are activated, your appetite might disappear as your body switches into fight-flight-or-freeze mode. Getting ready to ward off rivals, your heart rate quickens and your blood pressure spikes. You might sweat and feel a rush of heat and energy. Your eyes focus on and track potential threats. If you're jealous about a person, you may also look for signals that your special person is interested in your rival(s).

Thoughts

Jealous thoughts are basically worried thoughts with anger and agitation mixed in. When you feel jealous, your mind imagines losing a person or thing dear to you. You may try to come up with ways to stop or cope with this loss. Some scientists believe that jealousy is, in fact, a coping mechanism because it generates thoughts that may help you reinforce bonds and prepare yourself for potential loss.

Actions

Because jealousy stems from uncertainty that you can keep your relationships or possessions, jealous behaviors are often about trying to gain certainty. The problem with this is that certainty is impossible. As a result, jealous actions are often unrealistic attempts to tighten your grip. These behaviors might include invasive questioning; demanding attention, affection, or reassurance; trying to control others' interactions; being on high alert for rivals; and trying to keep the competition away. These actions could become aggressive and manipulative. You might also try to limit your own potential hurt feelings by abandoning or avoiding your treasured person or thing.

The Experience of Envy

Body Sensations

Envy has received relatively little attention from scientists, but this is changing as they begin to explore the ways this emotion plays out in the body and brain. A 2018 study made some important headway in this field.* In the experiment, researchers placed a pair of monkeys across from each other and rewarded them with sips of water for completing a simple task. While the monkeys sipped on their water, researchers scanned the monkeys' brains, focusing on the part of the brain that processes rewards. The monkeys' brains showed less of a reward response when their partner got a reward at the same time—even if the amounts of water were equal. These results indicated that the monkey valued its own water reward less when it saw its partner receiving the same reward. In other words, one monkey experienced less satisfaction from its reward because it was focused on what the other monkey got. Envy in action! You've probably seen envy in action in your own life. Imagine a small child playing with a toy. They lose interest in the toy when they notice another child with a similar toy.

---

* Noritake, Atsushi, Taihei Ninomiya, and Masaki Isoda. 2018. "Social Reward Monitoring and Valuation in the Macaque Brain." *Nature Neuroscience* 21: 1452–1462. doi.org/10.1038/s41593-018-0229-7.

You've probably seen envy in action in your own life. Imagine a small child playing with a toy. They lose interest in the toy when they notice another child with a similar toy.

Thoughts

Envious thoughts often focus on what you desire and how you can acquire it. You might think, "If only I had X, I would be so happy." You may imagine the desired thing or person or fantasize about having it or them. You might hatch plans to get what you want. You might also have angry or resentful thoughts about the person who possesses what you want or about how empty you feel without it. This anger is fueled by a feeling that your rival is better than you.

Actions

When you are envious, you believe the only way to rid yourself of this uncomfortable feeling is to get what you desire. Most people are too polite to directly take something or someone away from another person. They know this could lead to serious consequences. Therefore, people typically resort to trying to get their own version of the desired object or person. (Let's call this Plan A.) For example, if you envy a classmate's shoes, you may try your hardest to get a pair like that. Or if you think that person has a cool sweetheart, perhaps you can find a partner who seems similar. Are people usually happy with their own version of the "real thing"? Sometimes they are satisfied, yes—and sometimes the envy persists.

Another behavior strategy is to affiliate yourself with the person who has what you want. (Let's call this Plan B.) You may decide that if you cannot have what you want all to yourself, then perhaps you can gain some satisfaction by being close to or sharing it. When Plan A and Plan B are not possible or don't work, some people choose Plan C: denying that they want what they want, or even avoiding those who have it.

Jealousy and Envy Myths and Truths

Myth: Jealousy is a sign of love.

Truth: Some people think that if they're concerned that someone else may take their friend or partner from them, this means they have deep affection for the person. The reality is that love and jealousy are two different emotions. They can exist within an individual *simultaneously* and *separately*. They don't depend on each other. You could love someone *and* be jealous of them, or you could just love them. You should not excuse the inappropriate behaviors that sometimes come with jealousy by claiming that jealousy is a sign of your love. If you feel jealous when your friend or partner is talking to someone else, take a deep breath. Think about what your feelings are telling you. (See Three Questions to Understand Your Emotions on page 34.) Then decide how to behave responsibly. If you confuse jealousy with love, you might be missing important information that jealousy is telling you about yourself and your relationship.

Love and jealousy are two different emotions. You should not excuse the inappropriate behaviors that sometimes come with jealousy by claiming that jealousy is a sign of your love.

Myth: If I envy someone, it means I am a loser.

Truth: Envy can draw a stark contrast between what others have and what you have. When you look at others and see them with something you want, your mind can turn self-critical. You may start thinking you are not as good as the person you envy, and you may extend that to feeling generally worthless. This kind of self-assessment can be painful and may lead to even more difficult feelings, such as self-pity and shame. If you find yourself sliding down this slippery slope, remember that envy can be useful—but not for beating yourself up! Envy helps you identify resources and relationships that may bring long-term benefits to your life. You may not be able to get exactly what someone else has, and you definitely shouldn't try to take it from them, but you can use envy to become more focused, motivated, and energized to go out and get your own. Envy can lead you to a healthy sense of competition, which can in turn help you set and achieve goals that make you a better person.

Living with Jealousy

Jealousy can fill your head with thoughts and worries about losing someone or something you treasure. At its core, jealousy is a self-protective feeling, but it can also be damaging if it becomes all-consuming and puts you constantly on guard. If you're consumed with jealousy, you no longer experience the joy of the relationships and things you have. You can focus only on who is looking at them and whether you will lose them. All-consuming jealousy reflects your doubts and insecurities about yourself and whether you deserve what you have.

What good is it to be in a relationship with a wonderful person or have a wonderful thing when you spend all your time thinking about losing it? One way to deal with jealousy about a person is to accept that you have no control or authority over other people and remember that they are free to do as they wish. Loving someone does not give you the right to dominate their thoughts and actions. This truth can be scary for someone who feels jealous, but if you think hard about it, you'll realize that most people—perhaps including you—would say that a jealous friend or partner is an unattractive friend or partner. Of course, you can do nice things for your friend or partner to show your love and commitment, but if your actions are anything besides an expression of love, then your relationship is in trouble already.

You may also find yourself facing strong feelings of jealousy when your status in a group is threatened. Maybe a new girl, who is rumored to have a wicked jump shot, joins your basketball team. Or your best friend decides to run against you for student council treasurer. How do you handle the feeling that they may take your position and the attention that comes with it? Jealousy may have you focusing on what they are doing and how others are responding to it. But remember: jealousy reminds you of what you have and how important it is to you. Your jealous feeling is telling you that you value your standing in the group and all the social perks that come along with it. There's nothing wrong with that. A healthier response to your feelings in these situations is to embrace your desire to play great basketball or to win the election, and prepare yourself for some healthy competition. After all, you may come out on top, and if you don't, at least you can hold your head high for having faced the challenge honorably.

Living with Envy

It is not inherently problematic to want what someone else has. Envy can be a powerful source of motivation and goal setting. However, when your desire for another person's attribute, status, possession, or relationship becomes your primary focus, or when you want *exactly* what someone else has, not something *like* it, it's time to step back and think through your desires.

For example, perhaps your envy is not about wanting to be like someone else, but rather to *not* be yourself. Maybe you're overwhelmed by feelings of inferiority, and you see a solution to these uncomfortable feelings in being someone who has all the possessions, relationships, opportunities, status, and/or attributes that you don't currently have. While it can sometimes be healthy to emulate others, losing your own identity in the process is harmful.

Envy can distort your perception and thinking. When you feel envy, you don't know the full reality of having what you see someone else have. You may see only the benefits and overlook the challenges. You may also minimize what they have endured or sacrificed to get what you desire. Are you willing to make the same sacrifice? By asking yourself these questions, you may gain a healthier perspective on your desires.

Sometimes you may envy people because they have emotions you want. When you see them, they look carefree and happy— while you are bored, dissatisfied, sad, or angry. You may wish you were as happy as others seem to be. But can you be sure that they *feel* happy just because they *look* happy? After all, humans are skilled at feeling one way and behaving in another. In this situation, you are making the mental mistake of comparing your internal emotions with the external behaviors you observe in others. This is sometimes called "comparing your insides to somebody else's outsides." You see how someone behaves and assume the behavior is a true, complete expression of how they feel—when you really have no idea how they feel. The only way to know their feelings for certain is if the person tells you. If they haven't told you, don't put too much faith in your assumptions.

Thinking About Feeling

Have you ever seen a dog chasing a car and wondered what the dog would do if it caught the car? Does the dog even *want* to catch the car? Envy is a little like this. The focus is often on the chasing and not the catching. Think about a time when you envied someone you saw on social media. How would your life change if you had that person's attributes, features, relationships, or possessions? What might you gain? What might you lose?

CHAPTER 9
Guilt
and Shame

CRAIG AND ALEJANDRA'S STORY

Craig looked at Alejandra in shock. His eyes said it all. He could not believe she'd told a classmate that he was adopted. Nobody else at their school knew that his parents had adopted him as a baby. He had not told anyone because he'd only recently found out himself and was still processing his feelings about it. When he told Alejandra, he had sworn her to secrecy.

Alejandra could not have felt more ashamed of herself. Ugh—her big mouth! This was something she knew she had to work on. She had never been good with secrets, but the least she could have done is try a little harder to keep her mouth shut for Craig's sake. She could not even look at him. All she could do was stare at the floor.

● ● ● ●

There are some emotions that most people would just rather not have. These emotions are ones that make you feel uncomfortable, awkward, or plain old "bad." When you have these feelings, you may try your best to make them go away or cover them up with other feelings, such as anger.

Guilt and shame are two such emotions. Like jealousy and envy, guilt and shame are often confused with each other. They do share some traits, but they are different emotions. They reflect different experiences you may have with others and your world.

Guilt is regret or self-disapproval over a specific action. You may feel guilty when you believe you've done something wrong. You may believe your action—or inaction—has hurt another person physically or emotionally. You can also experience guilt when you do something that hurts yourself. For example, if you avoid studying for a test and you fail the test, you may feel guilty about choosing not to prepare. Finally, you might feel guilty when you've broken a rule or some other behavioral expectation—for example, when you don't complete your home-work or do your chores as your parent expects you to.

> Whereas guilt is regret about a specific behavior, shame is about devaluing your whole self.

You may experience guilt even when there's no consequence for your actions. It's almost as if the feeling itself is the conse-quence—a punishment for poor choices and behaviors. Many scientists believe that the function of guilt is to manage future behaviors. When you realize that you have behaved poorly, you are flooded with an emotion that is so unpleasant, you don't want to act that way ever again.

If that's guilt, then what is shame? Shame is a painful and overwhelming emotion you experience when you think you are "bad" or "not good enough." It may be triggered by something you've done, but shame goes further—into your core sense of yourself, not just your behavior. Whereas guilt is regret about a specific behavior, shame is about devaluing your whole self. When you feel shame, you believe you don't meet some standard that you or others have set for being a good or worthy person. You believe you are inadequate and inferior, and you fear that others may know it. Shame is about how you think others might see or judge you. Shame makes you feel unlovable and deserving of rejection. It is a judgment you pass on yourself that cannot be questioned or modified. Shame thoughts often start with the words *I am such a. . . .* The emotional weight of shame may make you want to hide or disappear. Whew—shame carries a lot of heavy, unpleasant baggage. If that negativity is weighing you down right now, you might want to take a breath to clear your head.

In its healthiest form, shame is an important emotion. It can help you assess yourself and identify changes that may help you live a better life. Shame makes you want to be acceptable to the people you care about. It makes you feel humble and motivates you to respect rules and boundaries. By making you feel terrible, shame helps you focus on ways you can change to connect better with others. Perhaps it is such a powerful feeling because social connection is so critical for humans. People need each other for physical and psychological well-being. Therefore, a strong negative experience, such as shame, can induce you to get back to being accepted by others.

The intensity of shame varies from a mild sense of feeling like a jerk to a severe sense of being a complete and utter failure. Embarrassment is a minor form of shame that you may experience when you do something specific that makes you look bad in front of others. To feel embarrassed, you need an audience—such as when you call someone the wrong name or when you trip and fall during gym class. Like guilt, embarrassment makes you feel bad about yourself for a specific behavior. But with embarrassment, you have not done wrong to yourself or someone else; you have usually just made a fool of yourself.

Shame is an emotion that brings you to a fork in the road. Down one road is self-punishment. This is where you feel the full intensity of the emotion. You loathe and pity yourself and sink under the weight of feeling like a person who sucks. This road is a path to pain. The other road leads to self-correction. This is where you experience the sting of social and personal judgment, but you don't get lost in it. You recognize that if you choose to make corrections and grow from the pain, you'll find relief. You give yourself another shot at meeting your own or others' expectations. Obviously, Self-Correction Boulevard is a healthier choice than Self-Punishment Avenue.

The Experience of Guilt

Body Sensations

The hallmark body sensation of guilt is a feeling of heaviness. You might feel as if you are carrying a weight inside you. You might hunch your shoulders, cast your eyes down or to the side, and move slowly.

Thoughts

When you feel guilty, you may find yourself replaying your wrong deed in your mind over and over. You may have self-critical thoughts and ask yourself, "Why did I . . . ?" You may also think about ways to make things right with the person you believe you've harmed (including if that person is you). If you can't come up with a solution, the problem may continue to spin around in your head. If you do come up with a solution, you may think obsessively about taking certain actions, such as apologizing, to improve the situation.

Actions

The behaviors that you may engage in when you feel guilty fall
into two categories: owning and avoiding. When you own your
feeling of guilt, you accept that you've done something wrong,
you take responsibility for your actions, and you are more likely
to act in ways that indicate repentance, such as apologizing.
When you avoid your feeling of guilt, you do not accept your
part in the harm that has occurred. This may cause you to
blame others, deny responsibility, or even be aggressive toward
people who trigger your guilty feelings.

The Experience of Shame

Body Sensations

People usually experience shame as a private emotion. When
it occurs in the context of other people, shame is often called
humiliation. When you feel humiliated, you believe people know
how "terrible" you are. The most common reaction to humiliation is the desire to hide. Sometimes people will describe this
desire by saying, "I wish the ground would open up and swallow
me." When the body experiences shame, it releases stress
hormones, making the body react as if it is under attack. These
chemicals cause your muscles to contract and your body to curl
up, perhaps to make you smaller and harder to see. You may
also avoid eye contact, feel hot in your upper body, and feel a
weight in your chest, causing your shoulders to droop.

Thoughts

When you feel shame, you have negative and judgmental
thoughts about yourself. You may also have self-critical
thoughts about your identity, taking one aspect of yourself—a
behavior or an attribute—and using that to conclude that you

are bad, unlovable, or unworthy. Shame may bring thoughts of hiding or running away from others. You might believe that others can see all your inadequacies and that they will judge or reject you.

Actions

Psychologist Linda Hartling suggests that shame causes people to behave in three specific ways:

Hiding is the first way. People who feel ashamed may try to reduce their terrible feelings by reducing their exposure to and contact with others. They may even dress and move in ways that make them less noticeable.

Appeasing and pleasing is the second way. This may play out as over-smiling, doing favors, or trying to be liked. When people feel that they do not deserve to be in a relationship or group, appeasing and pleasing behaviors are a way to make up with the person or group they feel has rejected them.

Moving against the perceived source of judgment and shame is the third way. Someone who feels ashamed may act aggressively—verbally or physically—against the person who triggered this shame. The person who feels ashamed may believe that if they can get rid of the person who triggered this emotion, then they can get rid of the shame itself.

Guilt and Shame Myths and Truths

Myth: I'll feel guilty only when I do something wrong to others.
Truth: Guilt applies not only to your behavior toward others, but also to things you did or didn't do for yourself. For example, have you ever felt guilty for oversleeping instead of working on a personal project? Letting yourself down can be as painful as not meeting others' expectations.

Myth: Shaming someone can make them change.

Truth: Shaming others is a common strategy for trying to change behavior. It involves making someone feel bad so they will want to feel better by behaving differently. Sometimes parents use this strategy. Making someone feel ashamed of a behavior can work, but only if the shamed person wants to change *and* the change is within their control. Shaming can backfire if it angers or provokes someone to double down on their behavior. Sometimes the shamed person may appear to change but really has just begun hiding the undesirable behavior. Shaming is particularly harmful when people cannot control or change what they are being shamed for, such as their physical features, mental health, identity, or something that happened long ago. In these cases, shaming is harassment. This is a favorite strategy of people who bully others. Whether shame works to change behavior is beside the point, though, because other strategies, such as encouragement, praise, and positive feedback, usually work better. Meanwhile, using shame to inspire change may have a hidden long-term cost. The person being shamed may change their behavior, but what if they internalize the shame? What if it continues to make them feel bad after they change their behavior? Is the change worth the damage done?

Living with Guilt

If you are struggling with feelings of guilt, it's important to ask yourself whether your mistake is fixable. Can you make it better? If so, then get to work! Perhaps you need to come clean, apologize, have a discussion, or develop new skills. That's what the feeling of guilt is moving you to do.

But what if you can't fix the problem? Maybe what you did wrong is too far in the past, it's beyond your control, or the damage has already been done. This is a tougher situation to deal with. You may find yourself feeling regret and thinking, "If only I had. . . . " Regret is a cousin to guilt, but it has more sadness and less self-directed anger. Regret can be difficult to manage because the only way to fix it is to go back in time and do something different—and of course, this is impossible. Instead of wishing for time travel, try self-compassion.

> When people do something wrong, they are often their own harshest critics; they are meaner to themselves than they would be to their worst enemies. How would you treat a good friend who is experiencing regret? Treat yourself with the same patience, tenderness, and warmth.

Self-compassion is a process in which you acknowledge your difficult thoughts, feelings, and memories and treat yourself with kindness. Painful feelings such as guilt and regret are part of the journey of human life. By remembering that you are human, you can take a broader view of your suffering. When people do something wrong, they are often their own harshest critics; they are meaner to themselves than they would be to their worst enemies. Self-compassion is doing the opposite— being more understanding toward yourself. How would you treat a good friend who is experiencing regret? Treat yourself with the same patience, tenderness, and warmth. This won't fix the mistake you made, but it'll help you do better in the future.

Living with Shame

Most teenagers encounter shame in their daily lives on social media. Social media platforms have become places where people post comments with the intention of making others feel bad about anything and everything—clothing choices, body size, disabilities, relationship decisions, personal life choices, and more. Sometimes the shaming becomes harassment and bullying. Countless young people have considered suicide or ended their lives in response to online harassment. Online shaming can be especially intense and unrelenting because the shamers can have some degree of anonymity when they post, and they don't have to witness the real-life impact their words have on others.

Apart from online shaming, teens experience plenty of other shame in their lives. It can be difficult to feel that you must meet all the expectations your culture puts on you: being attractive, being smart, having social status, having all the right things (technology, clothes, and other possessions), and so much more. What happens when you don't believe you're successful in any of these areas? You probably feel shame.

Remember that shame is usually an exaggeration in your mind. If you think about it rationally, are you really unworthy because you don't have the latest phone? Are you stupid because you failed a test? Are you damaged because your parents divorced? No. Shame can make you hyperaware of whether you are good enough to belong in a certain group, so one way to manage this distressing feeling is to ask yourself if you really want to be in a group that requires you to be "perfect" in any way. For example, if you feel some shame when you miss a goal in hockey, it is probably healthy insofar as it helps you focus on improving your game. But if this feeling of shame persists and intensifies and you always feel like crap, then shame is no longer healthy. It's not a motivator toward success but rather a hurtful force that holds you back.

Thinking About Feeling

If someone feels shame or guilt, they may have the urge to apologize. Think of a time when someone apologized to you, and you did not believe them. What was it about their words or tone that you didn't buy? Did you feel they were saying sorry just to feel less guilty or ashamed, or perhaps to silence you or get you to move on? What could they have done differently to convince you the apology was sincere? When you apologize, make sure you're doing it sincerely and for the right reasons.

CHAPTER 10
Happiness as Joy

MEERA'S STORY

Today was the day. Meera felt that she had done all she could do to get an A on her chemistry final exam, and her teacher would be handing back the graded tests this afternoon. She had studied hard, completed all her homework, and even gone to tutoring. It had been hard work, but she wanted to go on to college, and she knew she had to have strong grades. Plus, her mother had told her that if she improved her grades, she could visit her favorite aunt in Georgia for the summer.

Ms. Hill started handing back the exams. Some of the students were frowning and sighing as they saw their grades. Kobe got his exam and gave a half smile. He was smart; he probably got an A and felt bad because he didn't get an A+. Ms. Hill laid Meera's exam on her desk facedown. Meera paused for a second and then lifted it up. Her grade was an A. She felt a rush of pure joy. She had done it—she was so excited!

* * *

Of all the emotions we've discussed in this book, happiness is the most desired. It is the ultimate positive feeling. If you were to ask a large group of teens what they want most in life, the most popular answer would likely be some version of *to be happy*. But if you were to ask the same teens to describe what happiness means to them, you would get a wide range of answers: *money*, *pleasure*, *personal success*, *relationships*, *popularity*, and more. Among the many teens I've worked with over the years, nearly all had a general goal of being happier. However, the specifics of happiness depended on their circumstances and personalities. If so many people think about happiness in so many ways, then what is the common factor linking all these diverse goals?

Humans have been trying to answer this question since ancient times. Many great philosophers, such as Siddhartha Gautama (Buddha) of India, Confucius of China, Abu Hamid Al-Ghazali of Persia, and Aristotle of Greece, all took a shot at understanding happiness. They all came to different conclusions.

One important perspective to consider came from Aristotle, who explored happiness as a concept called *eudaemonia*. He saw eudaemonia (happiness) as the ultimate goal of life. Eudaemonia is a long-lasting state of serenity achieved at the end of life by engaging in virtuous actions, such as helping others, making healthy choices, and building strong relationships. Eudaemonia is the final outcome of a life well lived. This idea of happiness differs from another ancient Greek concept of happiness, called *hedonia*.

Hedonia is the positive feeling that comes from increasing the experience of pleasure (or fun) and decreasing the experience of pain (or boredom, frustration, sadness, or anxiety). Unlike eudaemonia, which is a long-lasting result of a lifetime of virtuous choices, hedonia is the immediate and short-lived result of pleasurable choices. The modern English word *hedonism* comes from the word *hedonia*. Hedonism is the pursuit of pleasurable or fun experiences while avoiding activities that might be stressful. An example of hedonistic behavior could be frequently hanging out and partying with friends while avoiding your schoolwork.

Current scholars have also considered these two perspectives of happiness. Psychologist Sonja Lyubomirsky, for example, offers a definition of happiness that combines both the immediate, short-lived components and the longer-lasting components of the emotion. She proposes in her book *The How of Happiness* that happiness is "the experience of joy, contentment, or positive well-being, combined with a sense that one's life is good, meaningful, and worthwhile." She argues that although these components are linked, they can be unique experiences too.

These are a lot of complex ideas. How can you make sense of it all? To make this information easier to understand and more useful, let's focus on the two components of happiness separately. This chapter will discuss happiness as experiencing pleasure or having things go the way you want, which is called *joy*. The next chapter will look at happiness as living a meaningful, fulfilling life, which is called *well-being*.

What Is Joy?

Joy is the intense, immediate, overwhelming feeling you have when things go your way. You may feel joy when your plans work out, when you are able to solve a problem, or when you get something you want. It makes you want to wave your arms, pump your fists, jump up and down, smile, laugh, shout, hug others, and sometimes cry as you experience the satisfaction of triumph. Joy is delight. It feels like "YAY!!!"

Joy, like other emotions, exists on a spectrum that includes excitement, delight, elation, awe, exultation, and more. Some people describe their experience of joy as magical—they feel as if they are somehow suddenly connected to people, places, or things in ways that they cannot explain. If you have ever stood at the top of a mountain or looked into a vast canyon or gazed at a starry sky, that feeling you experienced was probably joyful.

Joy is also what you experience when you are engaged in pleasurable activities, or when you are having fun. Pleasure is different from person to person; what pleases you depends on what interests you. For example, you might get pleasure from completing a puzzle, getting a good grade, winning a prize, attending a concert, getting a hug or kiss from someone you love, riding a roller coaster, or doing something new and challenging such as skydiving.

The word *hedonistic* means "pleasure-seeking." There is nothing inherently wrong with seeking pleasure, but hedonism can be harmful if you seek happiness at any cost. A search for joy may lead you to make harmful choices; avoid challenging but beneficial activities such as school, relationships, and a healthy lifestyle; or engage in cheap thrills such as drugs, alcohol, unhealthy eating, and unsafe sexual activity.

Joy can also be understood as the opposite of sadness. From this perspective, sadness is about losing people and things, and joy is about gaining or winning. It is how you feel when you succeed, as opposed to how you feel when you fail. When things go your way and you reach a desired goal, like Meera in the opening story of this chapter, you may experience a burst of emotion—that's joy. You may feel joy when you avoid pain too. Whenever you successfully conquer or sidestep stress or disaster, it can feel pleasurable. Have you ever thought you were going to fail a test and then you didn't? You may not have gotten the best possible grade, but seeing a passing grade on your paper probably got you up and doing a happy dance.

The Experience of Joy

Body Sensations

Joy produces complex and sometimes contradictory bodily reactions. You might both laugh *and* cry. Joy can leave you speechless, with a sense of deep, intense, quiet connection with another person or thing—or it may fill you with energy that inspires you to yell, hug, and engage with others. Scientists who have studied the brain when it is in a state of joy report important changes in a wide range of brain chemicals and brain activity. These diverse chemicals and types of activity are correlated with the many types of body reactions.

Thoughts

Scientists say that unpleasant emotions, such as anger and sadness, cause people to narrow their thoughts to focus on triggers or solutions. Pleasant emotions like joy seem to do the opposite. These emotions open up your thinking. Joy can inspire you to explore, connect, engage, and play, with no particular goal in mind. It moves you to try to be closer to the source of the pleasant feeling or other people, things, or situations that trigger the same feeling.

Actions

Joyful thoughts may encourage your involvement in activities, play, and exploration that you believe will bring you more joy. This could be exercise, athletics, interactions with others, intellectual pursuits, or artistic and creative expressions. As long as you are in a joyful state of mind, you will seek out these pleasure-producing actions. You might find yourself actively recalling the details of your success or wanting to tell the story to others over and over again. Joy breeds joyful behavior, and joyful behavior breeds more joy.

Joy Myths and Truths

Myth: Material things will bring you joy.

Truth: The degree to which material things impact your sense of joy depends a lot on your socioeconomic class. Wealthier people tend to value experiences over material things, because they already have access to a lot of stuff, and their basic needs have been met. People with less income enjoy experiences too, but some may find more pleasure in material things because those can have a large and immediate impact on their lives.

Myth: You can get pleasure from drugs and alcohol.

Truth: One of the most common ways that humans try to experience pleasure is through using drugs and alcohol. Since ancient times, people have been using various substances to achieve a high, which is a temporary experience of pleasant emotions (or a temporary decrease in negative emotions). Many people try out drugs and alcohol for the first time during adolescence. So, if it's such a common part of human culture, then what's the big deal about using drugs and alcohol? After all, in most societies alcohol is legal, and drugs such as marijuana are becoming legal too. Some major concerns are that inappropriate use may lead to addiction or harm brain development. When drugs are prescribed and administered by a medical professional with years of training and experience, they can be helpful in addressing medical and mental health conditions. But when any drug is obtained or used without expert supervision or guidance, the risk of physical harm or addiction increases considerably. Addiction occurs when your brain becomes dependent on a constant flow of the drug or alcohol. Then you need to increase the amount you take to get the same high, and your body goes through a withdrawal phase of illness if you stop using the drug. Addiction is associated with many harmful outcomes, including damage to the brain and body, relationship tension and loss, problems with the law, overdose, and death.

Living with Joy

Joy is triggered by pleasurable activities, so to experience this emotion, you need to engage in things that bring you pleasure. If you know what brings you pleasure and you are not pursuing it, then you are limiting the experience of joy in your life. Make a list of five activities that you find pleasurable, and set specific, regular times when you can engage in those activities. This may require some coordination with others, but the joy will be worth the work.

Even the process of working toward a pleasurable activity can be pleasurable in itself. Let's say that you have an interest in painting. Perhaps due to school and your part-time job, you have not been able to paint as much as you'd like. One way to activate joy in relation to painting is to plan and schedule a time when you could paint again. Perhaps when the school year ends? In the meantime, you could visit websites that show new painting techniques and art tools. You can make small notes on what you could paint next and sketch out ideas. You could even visit art galleries and talk to friends about paintings that you enjoy. These small steps, even if they are not the full expression of what you want to do, will surely bring you small moments of joy.

You may find that, try as you might, no joyful activities come to mind. Maybe you haven't had many enjoyable experiences. Maybe you know what you enjoy doing, but you cannot actively participate. Perhaps you are depressed, stressed, or anxious and so overwhelmed by these feelings that you cannot identify or participate in pleasurable activities. You may feel numb or disconnected from the world and your own life. Even in situations where other people find joy, you might feel removed and distant. If any of this sounds familiar, I strongly encourage you to talk about it with an adult who can help you with your emotions. You can begin by identifying someone you trust and respect, such as a teacher, guidance counselor, coach, clergyperson, parent, or other relative. Let them know that you would like to set some time aside to talk with them about your thoughts and feelings. Scheduling the talk will allow the adult to be more prepared, focused, and ready to listen. They may be able to give you perspective, advice, or guidance. They may even be able to connect you with a professional mental health counselor. If you cannot identify an adult to talk with, you still have options. For example, there are many phone-based support services called warmlines (for nonemergencies) and hotlines (for emergencies) that you could reach out to. Each state has a version of this service. Visit nami.org to find those in your area. You can also call or text 988, a new suicide and crisis lifeline available throughout the United States. It provides confidential support 24 hours a day, seven days a week to people in suicidal crisis or mental health-related distress.

Thinking About Feeling

Can you remember an activity you did as a child just for the fun of it? Most likely, no one made you do it or rewarded you for doing it. Try to engage in a version of this activity now. For example, maybe you loved putting on plays with friends or siblings when you were little. Why not try out for a school or community play? You might rediscover the same joy you felt years ago.

CHAPTER 11
Happiness as Well-Being

IMANI'S STORY

Imani sat on her porch sipping lemonade. It was chilled just enough to help her tolerate the summer heat, but not enough to irritate her sensitive teeth. She looked out over the lawn toward the cars that quietly drove by. She felt good. This was a little surprising, because a lot of major changes had happened in her life during the past year. Her parents had divorced, her boyfriend had broken up with her, and she had not been accepted to her first-choice college. She had cried a lot of tears over these "failures." But she still felt good. The divorce had helped her finally see that her parents had never really been happy together. Her own breakup helped her realize that her ex was asking for more than she was willing to give at this point in her life. And going to the local state college was not so bad. It was cheaper than a private school, and her favorite teacher, Ms. Torres, had gone there and loved it. Yes, she definitely felt good. She was feeling strong, clear, and engaged with her life. She had many uncertainties, for sure, but she also felt that she had learned a lot in the past year, and she was ready for whatever the future brought. She took another sip of lemonade, sighed, and smiled to herself.

As discussed earlier, happiness is a broad category that captures multiple related but distinct feelings. As Sonja Lyubomirsky describes, the first component of happiness is an immediate positive response to pleasurable events or things going your way. The ancient Greeks called this kind of happiness hedonia. I call it joy and discussed it in chapter 10.

The second component Lyubomirsky identifies is a bit more sophisticated. It is the subtle and sustained sense that your life is good, meaningful, and worthwhile. It's when you are not just *feeling* good but when you feel that your life *is* good—you are living in a way that challenges you and brings out the best in you. You are not stuck in the past or worrying about the future but living life to its fullest in the present moment. This is not a perfect life, but a satisfying one—a life that makes you feel alive and . . . well . . . happy. Aristotle called this type of happiness eudaemonia. I call it well-being. It feels like "Aaahhh."

What Is Well-Being?

If joy is how you feel when you get what you want or something good happens, such as scoring a point while playing a team sport, well-being is how you feel when you're happy being a part of the team and playing a sport you enjoy. Even if you are not the best player, you feel satisfaction with contributing and being challenged and engaged. This type of happiness is not about accomplishment; it is about connection.

You experience well-being when you're living a life that feels right—when your happiness is connected to experiences that matter to you. Consider this thought experiment proposed by the philosopher Robert Nozick: You are given the option to lie in bed all day and be hooked up to a machine that will give you an endless supply of happy feelings. Would you want to spend the rest of your life connected to this machine? My guess is that after some thought, you would say no. There would be something missing from this experience—even if you felt happy all the time—because it would include no meaningful activity.

Well-being is not about everything going well. In fact, people who feel well-being have their share of misfortune, challenge, and stress. They struggle just like anyone else, but they are engaged in activities that they value highly and gain satisfaction from that.

> People who feel well-being have their share of misfortune, challenge, and stress. They struggle just like anyone else, but they are engaged in activities that they value highly and gain satisfaction from that.

Lyubomirsky and her colleagues have proposed that happiness is determined partly by biology and genetics, partly by life circumstances, and partly by intentional activities (choices and actions). Here's an example to help you think about how these factors contribute to happiness. Consider two students, Keisha and Tyrell, who compete on debate teams at two different high schools in the same area. Since birth, both have tended to be optimistic and hopeful. Both have always loved learning and talking about things that are happening in the world. (These characteristics are genetics at work.) Once they got to high school, each sought out opportunities to join their school's debate team. (This is choice and action.) At one debate tournament, they competed against each other directly. Tyrell's team won, and Keisha's team lost. (These are life circumstances.) When asked how happy they are right after the tournament, Tyrell says he's pumped, and Keisha says she's bummed. In other words, Tyrell feels joyful; Keisha, not so much. When asked again a week later, they both say they're happy. They are both still engaged in an activity they enjoy—they love the competition, camaraderie, and challenge. Their choice to stay involved in debate, which they value highly, goes beyond the circumstance of winning or losing and brings them both a sense of well-being.

So how can you live a life that produces feelings of well-being? Scientists have been studying this question for some time now, and they have come up with some suggestions. One factor that strongly influences well-being is personal values.

Personal Values

Personal values, for our purposes, are your strongly desired, freely chosen life direction. They are your deeply felt sense of what is important in your life. Your values define how you want to relate to yourself, others, and the world. Values are not moral, religious, or ethical rules (although they can be guided or influenced by these concepts), but rather what you want your life to be about. Values are the path *you* want to walk on in your life. Here are some important things to know about values.

> Values are the path you want
> to walk on in your life.

A personal value is not a thing or a person, but an action. Often when people are asked about their values, they talk about specific objects or people. They may say they value their dog or their friends or money. These are not values, but rather objects of someone's values. Values are a person's free choice about how they want to *be with* the people and things in their lives. So, the values in the dog, friend, and money examples might be "loving my pet unconditionally," "having great adventures with my friends," or "making money." These statements reflect relationships and interactions rather than objects or people.

Personal values are not static; they can change over time. Your values as a teen may shift as you grow into an adult. But at every point in your life, your values will feel real, meaningful, and personal, especially when you are actively living your life based on them. Understanding yourself may be a value that's motivating you to read this book now, as a teenager. If you become a parent someday, you may read this book again because one of your values is understanding your children.

You can have different personal values for different aspects of your life. For example, as a student you may want to be focused and hard-working, and as a friend you may want to be kind and patient. You will be able to keep these values separate and work on them independently most of the time, but sometimes they may come into conflict. For example, what if your friend is in your history class and keeps trying to talk to you while you are doing an assignment? You may have to choose between being the patient friend or the focused student.

Values are strongly desired. A personal value is something that no one has to tell you. You just know. In my work with young people, I ask them to tell me how it feels to talk about their values. Often they say that they feel "uplifted" or "inspired" or "motivated." Your personal values resonate deep within you, and you never need to be convinced about your belief in them. They're a bit like your favorite flavor of ice cream. There are countless flavors of ice cream, but even with all these options, you probably have a favorite. You don't have to be convinced to like your favorite flavor. You just know it when you taste it!

Personal values are not goals. In fact, goals come from values. Goals are specific outcomes that you can achieve as you live out your values. You can live out your values in your life by setting small, medium, and big goals. You can achieve a goal and then check it off your list, but you can never achieve a value because you continue to live out your value over time. Put another way, a value is your path and your goal is one of the many steps you take along the path. For example, if your value is to be famous, one goal might be to create a product that millions of people will want to buy. Another goal could be going to college and getting a degree in engineering so you gain the skills to create this amazing product. You can come up with endless goals to put on your to-do list to help you manifest your value of being famous. The clearer your values, the clearer the goals you can set.

As important as it is to *know* your personal values, you cannot achieve the true emotional experience of well-being until you *live out* these values. Well-being happens when you *act* on your values. When you identify your values, it is important to state them as ongoing actions that you can do in small, medium, and big ways. For example, you may believe that love is important, but love is not in itself a personal value. You could describe love as a value through the phrase *showing love to my family*. This phrase starts with an action word. It also captures the idea that your value can be expressed and acted upon in a million and one ways. It is in the *doing* of the action, or working on a values-based goal (doing one of your parent's usual chores, giving hugs to your grandma, spending quality time with your sibling) that you reap the real emotional benefit of values. Well-being! Happiness!

Values and Well-Being

Values bring a range of benefits that lead to a happier, more content life. Let's take a look at some of them.

Values give you focus. *Once you are facing the right direction, all you have to do is keep walking.* This saying captures the positive impact clear values can have on a person. When you know what is important to you and how you want to live, you have the freedom and focus to simply take steps in that direction. Values help you avoid getting confused or distracted by unrelated thoughts, feelings, and situations. You can keep your eyes on the prize and just keep working toward it. Here's an example from my own youth. My favorite pastime when I was a child and teenager was drawing superheroes. I read tons of comic books and graphic novels and tried to come up with my own heroes and villains. I loved to get a nice, sharp pencil and a blank sheet of paper and create a brand-new superhero. I would immerse myself in drawing the character's face, mask, and costume, using all kinds of colors to draw the glowing fists or shimmering weapons. It was awesome! I had a deep passion for drawing and storytelling, and when I was working on my comic books, all my other teenage concerns would melt away. It was not only fun; it also made me very happy.

Values give you purpose. Country musician Dolly Parton once said, "Find out who you are and do it on purpose." Your values explain who you are, and acting on your values is the path to wholeness, completeness, and happiness. When you are clear on your values, they can give you a strong sense of purpose and meaning in your life.

Values help you make decisions. Knowing your values does not make life a piece of cake. You will face challenges and you will have to make critical choices. How will you make up your mind? By checking your values, of course!

Your values give context to your problems and their possible solutions. Values give you a way of weighing the options and deciding what to do. Here's another example from my childhood. When I was 12 years old, I had the opportunity to apply to an excellent middle school. Many of my friends also wanted to go to this school, and I knew that it would be a good step toward preparing me for college. To get ready for the entrance exam, I knew that I would have to beef up my math skills. I was pretty good in math, but I wanted to feel more confident for the exam and knew I'd have to study over the summer to get there. This was a tough decision for me, because I really enjoyed hanging out with my buddies and playing basketball in the summer. We had so little time to just hang out during the school year. But as much as I enjoyed my friends, I truly valued being a strong student. I clearly saw myself going to college, and I knew I needed to work hard to be a good student. So, I decided to ask my father to help me brush up on my math skills that summer. My dad was an engineer, so he was very good at math. My decision wasn't easy, but it was *easier* because I was able to look at my options through the lens of my values. My values helped me be willing to sacrifice hours of summer basketball fun to spend time doing algebra and geometry worksheets. That summer was a struggle, but the struggle was meaningful, and that made me feel content.

People with strong values tend not to worry about what others think of them, because they realize, "I have my own path, and others have theirs."

Values give you self-confidence. Another benefit of values is that they help you believe in yourself. People who know what they want and what lights their fire usually feel safe and secure in themselves. They focus on what actions they can take to continue being the person they want to be. People with strong values tend not to worry about what others think of them, because they realize, "I have my own path, and others have theirs." Have you ever met someone who knew what they loved and spent a lot of time doing it? Did they seem confident? I remember many students from my high school days whom others thought were nerds because they spent a lot of time playing video games. Some students often made fun of them and mocked their interests. But these so-called nerds hardly ever cared what others said. They knew what they loved, and they had friends who shared those values. They would talk endlessly and excitedly about the new games they were playing and what levels they had reached. They had no time to listen to haters; they were having too much fun.

Values help you form stronger, healthier relationships. A former client of mine, Tricia, came to see me when she was 18 because she was struggling with severe social anxiety.

TRICIA'S STORY

When we started working together, Tricia had just gotten accepted into college. She was excited about being a college student and studying her favorite subjects. At the same time, she was experiencing a high level of dread and worry about moving into a residence hall and living with other people. She was used to spending time alone. She'd had few friends, and these relationships usually didn't last long because she would become overwhelmed with anxious thoughts of rejection and eventually cease contact.

Our work together focused on how Tricia could manage her anxiety well enough to move onto campus. She'd cautiously begun communicating with her new roommate by text, but these interactions often left Tricia exhausted from stress. Each text she sent or received brought on a litany of overanalysis, worried thoughts, and nervous feelings. "What if my text is too long? What if she thinks I'm weird? What if I embarrass myself? Why does she want to know my interests?" It was all Tricia could do to not cancel her plans to stay on campus.

Move-in day finally came. We had prepared as well as we could, but I was still only 50 percent sure that Tricia would stay past the first weekend. She moved in on Friday and was back at home with her parents by Sunday night.

After celebrating that she gave it a try, we both buckled down to see what more we could do about her struggles. One of the things I pointed out to Tricia, as we talked about her feelings, was that the anxiety she felt indicated that she loved people and wanted connections with them. It showed that connecting with others was a personal value for her. After all, if she didn't care about having friends, she wouldn't be anxious about rejection; she would be nonchalant or indifferent. But she liked people, so she cared what they thought about her.

As we talked more, I helped Tricia understand that anxiety's job is to keep people safe from emotional and physical harm, not to make them happy. Happiness requires risk. She would have to step outside her comfort zone to make friends. I asked her bluntly, "Are you willing to risk rejection to make meaningful connections with others?" She struggled with this question for a while, but eventually decided to take action.

By the time we concluded our work together, Tricia had moved into a single bedroom on campus (a first step toward sharing a room with someone else), joined some clubs, and made some friends. She'd found other students who shared some of her interests (horror movies, international foods, and writing short stories) and connected with them. Her anxiety still flared sometimes, but overall she was much happier and more content. She had acknowledged her values and her deep desire to make friends and was taking steps in this direction. It made all the difference for her.

* * * *

Tricia's story is a rather extreme example of how values can affect relationships, but it does show clearly how values can give you the focus and energy you need to develop relationships and reciprocate positive feelings with friends. Your values can also help you keep your relationships healthy by giving you a common ground upon which to assess your connections. Tricia met many new students as she explored and built her social life, and the work that we did during this time included finding out if she wanted to continue her relationships with some of them. The way we worked through these decisions was by returning to her values. How did Tricia want to be in the context of friendships? She said she wanted to form friendships that were supportive and safe, where she could enjoy good times but also find understanding when things got bad. We used this value as a lens to look at her connections with new acquaintances and determine how much time and energy she wanted to commit. This lens gave her a healthier perspective on rejection. It was more tolerable for Tricia to perceive unsuccessful connections as due to different values rather than her being weird or unlikeable.

Values and Flow

Let's say you are an artist who loves to draw. One of your personal values is getting better at drawing. To live out this value, you schedule three times a week to work on your drawing skills. Imagine you're sitting at a table working on a drawing you've been thinking about for weeks. It's an image of a woman holding a flower. You've selected your pencils and paper and you are sitting in a comfortable chair. You begin to draw. It is a slow, careful process, and you are fully absorbed. Your brain, eyes, and hands are fully coordinated. You render each line and contour with ease, and the picture is coming together effortlessly. You do not get tired, hungry, or bored. You are fully focused and dedicated to your craft. The drawing is not perfect, but you continue working at it, because you have confidence in your skills. How would you describe such an experience? Scientists would say that in that moment, you are "in the flow."

Engaging in values-based activities can put you in a state of flow. Flow is a state of full immersion in a meaningful and challenging activity. The activity usually has a clear goal, and you believe that your skills match the requirements of the task. Flow is a balance between frustration, which happens when the difficulty is too high, and boredom, which happens when the difficulty is too low. Flow can occur during work, sports, play, socializing, or even during relaxation. Flow feels like a state of timelessness and personal satisfaction. You are engaging in the activity not because you have to or someone is expecting you to, but for the pure fulfillment and value of it. Being in the flow makes you feel "strong, alert, in effortless control, unselfconscious, and at the peak of [your] abilities," as described by Mihaly Csikszentmihalyi, a researcher in happiness and creativity. Doesn't that sound like happiness? What activity puts you in a state of flow? And how do you feel when you engage in that activity?

Values and Self-Care

Life can be hard. It is filled with many challenges and obstacles. If you are trying to live your values and achieve well-being, it is important that you take care of yourself. Self-care is intentionally doing things that improve your emotional and physical health and functioning. In other words, self-care is what you do to recharge your batteries. When you prioritize your health, you make well-being, or flow, possible. As the saying goes: *you can't pour from an empty cup; you must fill it first.* Self-care is how you keep your emotional and physical health cup filled up.

Are you taking the time to care for yourself emotionally and physically? For an activity to be self-care, it has to go beyond being fun, exciting, or relaxing. Coming home from school and plopping on your bed with your phone to watch your favorite shows for three hours may be fun, but does it recharge your batteries? Maybe, maybe not. It takes your mind off school, but it also gets in the way of homework. How about staying out past your curfew with your friends? It may be exciting, but is it self-care? Does it fill your cup?

Here are some guidelines to help you figure out whether an activity is truly self-care:

- Your intention must be to improve or maintain your health.

- You plan the activity and engage in it regularly.

- Your activity isn't necessarily fancy or expensive.

- The self-care aspect of the activity is unique to you.

Let's look at sleep, for example. Getting a regular eight to nine hours of sleep each night is a healthy practice for a teenager. However, for some teens, it may also be self-care to sleep late on Sunday mornings and get more than ten hours of rest. Or how about exercise? Going to the gym and taking an aerobic dance class once a week sounds like good self-care. To be good *physical* self-care, though, it can't be just walking around the gym chatting with friends. Another example is shopping. A planned afternoon outing to the mall with friends can be a relaxing, fun, and battery-charging activity. However, impulsively buying jeans when you really can't afford them may leave you anxious and stressed when you look at your bank account later on. Self-care can be many things, but remember that the activity should improve your life and move you toward, not away from, well-being.

The Experience of Well-Being

Body Sensations

Like all emotions, well-being produces effects both inside and outside your body. Like joy, well-being may cause you to smile, laugh, and grin. However, the real benefit is on the inside. The happiness you feel inside your body is related to the release of "happy hormones." These include dopamine, which is associated with pleasurable sensations, memory, and learning; endorphins, which are a natural pain-reliever; and serotonin, which helps regulate bodily functions such as sleep, appetite, and digestion. Healthy physical habits such as getting enough sleep, eating wisely, and regular exercise support well-being and encourage the release of happy hormones.

Thoughts

Whereas stress can trigger negative, narrow, rigid thinking, well-being usually leads to broader, more positive, and more flexible thinking. Stressed people don't have the brain space to consider many options and tend to engage in black-and-white thinking. This means they are likely to limit their options to two extremes (black or white) and leave no space for the many more realistic options (gray) in between. For example, when I am overworked and not taking care of myself, I tend to see myself as either a success or a failure. I'm so stressed that my brain can see only those two options. However, when I am rested and engaging in positive, healthy activities regularly, I can think more flexibly. I can consider different possibilities in the gray area between failure and success. I can deal with the fact that sometimes I fail and sometimes I succeed, but overall I am still helping my clients. This makes me feel happier.

Actions

The Dalai Lama, spiritual leader of Tibetan Buddhists, says that "happiness isn't something ready-made; it comes from your own actions." When you work on and experience well-being, it leads to confidence. And when you are confident, you are open to taking calculated risks and engaging with the world in meaningful ways. These risks also tend to be true expressions of yourself. You are able to identify your chosen path and commit to walking that path with energy and purpose.

Well-Being Myths and Truths

Myth: Self-care and well-being are about achieving the perfect body.

Truth: There's no such thing as perfection (physical or otherwise). If you were to formulate your sense of well-being by looking at advertisements, you would think that unless you're dressed in stylish clothes with a perfectly toned body, doing yoga poses while smiling with flawless teeth, you are not doing it right. The image of self-care as an achievement of beautiful perfection is harmful. It sends the message that you have to be perfect while taking care of yourself or, worse, that the goal of taking care of yourself is attaining physical perfection. Both of these messages are wrong. Well-being is about everyone, of all body sizes and types, engaging in activities that improve mental, physical, and social functioning. Self-care is not always easy, but it is necessary. The goal of self-care is not to look great, but rather to use exercise and other body-and-mind care activities to stay healthy. Participation and dedication to your health makes you beautiful, not the outcome of this activity.

Myth: Self-care is a reward for accomplishing a goal.
Truth: This myth is based on the erroneous belief that self-care should be fun or relaxing and therefore must be earned. But self-care is not about pleasure. Rather, it is about activities that recharge your batteries when they're run down from the stresses of life. Self-care should be an important and regular part of a healthy lifestyle, not an incentive for completing difficult tasks. Self-care may boost your confidence and mood and improve your relationships with others, but fun is not the exclusive goal. In fact, some forms of self-care may be challenging—and not fun at all. For example, unplugging from social media may be really difficult for some people. These platforms are rich sources of information, connection, and entertainment, but excessive hours of screen time can harm your health and well-being. Therefore, taking a break—as hard as it may be—is an important act of self-care.

Living with Well-Being

YOUR STORY: TO FOLLOW OR TO CHOOSE

Imagine you are standing in a wide, flat field that extends to the horizon in every direction. There is not much in this field but grass and a few trees. You are alone and carrying a bag. This bag contains all the memories, stresses, and worries of your life. It is heavy with the weight of your life experiences. You look around and realize that you have 360 degrees of choice in which direction to go. You can go in any direction you want, but this abundance of options is confusing and overwhelming you. Then you hear a voice. The voice is kind but commanding. You cannot ignore it and feel compelled to obey it. The voice tells you to pick up your bag and head west. You look westward. It seems no different from any other direction, but you're glad for the command because it relieves your confusion. You decide to listen to the voice and begin walking, carrying your bag. After walking five miles, you stop to rest. You realize that despite all your walking, you are no closer to anything interesting. You look around. The scenery has changed somewhat, but you are not moved by anything you see. Your journey starts to seem pointless. And your bag feels so heavy!

After walking another five miles, you suddenly realize that you have been trudging along simply because a voice told you to. This voice is not familiar, but you decided to obey it anyway. It was nice to have someone make a decision for you, but now you realize that you gave up your right to choose your own path. This realization fills you with frustration and annoyance. Amid your anger, you also start to feel empowered. You realize that you can, in fact, decide which direction you want to go. It is scary to take matters into your own hands, but it's also invigorating to claim your autonomy. So, you set down your bag and take a seat next to it. You spend a few minutes listening to your deepest self. You start to feel an urge to walk southeast. Southeast just seems true. It seems . . . you. This renewed sense of direction fills you with confidence and energy. You jump to your feet, grab your bag, and turn to face southeast. The view is not that different from when you were walking west, but something about this path calls to you and makes you feel hopeful. You take a deep breath and begin to walk. Every step fills you with energy and your bag feels lighter because you're walking a path *you* chose that feels right to *you*.

♦ ♦ ♦ ♦

The happiness people seek often comes when they identify and engage in values-based activities. Once you figure out your values and act on them, you will begin to experience the satisfaction and contentment that lie at the core of happiness. To get you on this path as quickly as possible (if you are not on it already), let's talk a bit about how to identify your values. Here is one strategy that I often use in counseling.

Imagine that you are 80 years old, and your friends and family are throwing you a grand party. At this party, everyone you love is present. In fact, because this is an imaginary party, even people who have died or haven't yet been born are there. Everyone is in great spirits and eating, drinking, talking, and dancing. You look around at everyone and you are filled with pride and joy. One of your relatives who is hosting the event asks everyone to quiet down and invites guests to take the microphone and talk about the honoree: you. What would you like your friends and family to say about you—the kind of person you have been and how you have lived your life, how you have related to yourself, to them, and to the world? Make a list of what you'd love them to say about you. This list represents your values.

Now review your list and ask yourself if you are living out any of those values right now in your life. In big, small, or medium ways, are you making choices that reflect these values? Have you set goals based on your values? If you have, then good for you! You are probably experiencing some of the happiness you desire. Keep it up! If you are not, then now's the time to start. Set some goals that capture the essence of your values and begin working on them. For example, if you imagined that you'd want people to say you are caring, then set some goals for engaging in caring behaviors. These goals can be as small as giving a family member a hug today or as big as starting a club in your school that raises awareness about homeless veterans. It's up to you! But whatever you choose to do, knowing your values and working on them will fill you with well-being and other positive emotions.

Thinking About Feeling

This book covers a range of emotions that teens experience, but it just scratches the surface. There are so many other important feelings! Which ones come to your mind? Boredom? Loneliness? Excitement? Pride? As you work on being a healthy, emotional teen, think about your life and some of these other feelings. Which one would you like to focus on? You can use the structure of this book as a guide to better understand the emotion. Investigate the myths and truths around this feeling. What body sensations, thoughts, and actions are associated with it? And most importantly: what is the message the emotion conveys, and how you can use that data to reach your goals?

A FINAL WORD
Be an Emotional Teen

Adults often call teens "emotional"—in a critical and judgmental way. This putdown suggests that teenagers are easily overwhelmed or blinded by feelings and can't control their reactions or remain rational and sensible. You may hear this statement from adults who want you to "get a grip" or "snap out of it" and "use your brain." They assume that if you could just put aside or ignore your feelings, you would be more effective and successful in the situation you're facing. You might also hear such criticism from peers who are uncomfortable with your emotional reaction in a situation, whether it's crying, yelling, asking questions, shutting down, or something else. Peers' discomfort may lead them to mock your display of emotions. If you get such responses from others, you may become uneasy with emotions and willing to do anything to ignore, suppress, or reject them.

I hope that learning details about several common emotions has made you question the critics of emotional teens. Instead of seeing emotions as tricky things to be hidden or avoided, I hope you now see them as useful sources of information for improving your life. Paying attention to your feelings, whether pleasant or unpleasant, is more of a help than a hindrance to healthy and successful living.

Emotions get more overwhelming and uncontrollable when you try to control, change, or get rid of them. Difficult feelings can feel worse and can influence your actions more negatively when you resist them. For example, let's say you felt guilty because you didn't wash the dishes. Your mom confronted you about it, and you got defensive and started to mouth off and say you'd "get to it later." What was the real problem in this scenario? Was it about your mom reminding you of a chore you knew you had to do but didn't do? Or was it really about the unpleasant feeling of guilt that came over you when your mom pointed out the dishes piling up in the sink? Because you didn't like that feeling and wanted it gone as quickly as possible, you turned against the person you felt was causing it: your mom. Your guilty thoughts told you that if you could chase her away with some snarky words and weak explanations, the guilty feeling would go away too. But did it? No. Instead, your situation got worse.

Now imagine that instead of avoiding your guilt, you decided to "be emotional" and listen to the feeling you were experiencing. What might you learn from your feeling of guilt? As discussed in chapter 9, guilt is an unpleasant emotion that lets you know you've done something wrong. It usually shows up when you haven't behaved up to your own or others' expectations. It is so unpleasant that it may make you want to change your behavior so you don't experience that feeling again. By giving you an unpleasant emotional experience, guilt reminded you that you needed to fix your mistake and do better next time. Letting yourself feel the emotion of guilt taught you that the best way to keep this uncomfortable feeling at bay is to be true to your word. The dishes are your responsibility, and following through on your responsibilities is important. This example shows how being truly emotional and listening to your feelings can help you grow and be successful.

Now that you've read this book and have a new understanding of emotions, maybe "being emotional" can have a new meaning in your life. It can mean listening to your feelings. It can mean paying attention to the message that an emotion carries, and if you find that message helpful, using it to improve your life. Gone are the days of running away from your emotions, pleasant or unpleasant.

I encourage you to keep finding ways to open up to your internal experiences and use them to your benefit. Your emotions are sources of information you can use to make decisions and gain wisdom in your life, and it would be a missed opportunity to not harness this power. Go forth and be a powerful, emotional teen!

Index

A

action tendencies, emotions as having, 38–39

actions
  associated with anger, 54–55
  associated with anxiety, 71
  associated with envy, 79–80
  associated with guilt, 89
  associated with jealousy, 77–78
  associated with joy, 99
  associated with love, 46–47
  associated with shame, 90
  associated with well-being, 119
  emotions as combination of sensations, thoughts, and actions, 22–25
  emotions as expressed through actions, 24

addiction, 100

adolescence
  biological changes during, 16
  cognitive changes during, 16
  social changes during, 17

adrenaline, 53

alcohol, 41, 60, 98

Alejandra's story, about guilt and shame, 85

Al-Ghazali, Abu Hamid, on happiness, 96

all-or-nothing thinking, as example of ANTs, 71

Amal's story, about sadness, 59

Amen, Daniel (clinical researcher and psychiatrist), on ANTs (automatic negative thoughts), 71

Angela's story, about dealing with moving, 37–38

anger
  actions associated with, 54–55
  as basic human emotion, 51
  body sensations associated with, 53
  as having visible facial expressions and body movements, 44
  myths and truths about, 55
  role of, 51–52

strategies for living with, 56–57
  as substitute emotion/cover-up emotion, 52–53
  thoughts associated with, 53–54

anger management, 55

ANTs (automatic negative thoughts), 71

anxiety
  actions associated with, 71
  body sensations associated with, 70
  described, 67–68, 69–70
  as different from fear, 68
  management of, 73
  myths and truths about, 72
  purpose of, 7
  relationship of stress to, 68–69
  role of, 73
  thoughts associated with, 70–71

Anxiety and Depression Association of America, 72

appeasing, as behavior caused by shame, 90

Aristotle, on happiness, 96

automatic negative thoughts (ANTs), 71

B

"being emotional," meaning of, 127

blame, as example of ANTs, 71

body language, as conveying emotions, 23, 34

body sensations
  associated with anger, 53
  associated with anxiety, 70
  associated with envy, 78–79
  associated with guilt, 88
  associated with jealousy, 77
  associated with joy, 99
  associated with love, 45–46
  associated with sadness, 60–61
  associated with shame, 89
  associated with well-being, 118
  emotions as expressed through, 22–23

brain
  development of, 16

impact of stress on, 118–119
as producing hormones, 45, 49
breathing (deep), as strategy for living
with anger, 55, 56–57
Buddha (Siddhartha Gautama), on
happiness, 96

C

chicken-and-egg relationship, 68–69
childhood, 15–16
clinical depression, 62
communication, 26–27
conflict resolution, 55
Confucius, on happiness, 96
constructive angry acts, 54–55
Craig's story, about guilt and shame, 85
crush, defined, 47
crying
    myth and truth about, 62–63
    role of, 60–61
Csikszentmihalyi, Mihaly, on happiness
and creativity, 116

D

Dalai Lama, on happiness, 119
Darwin, Charles, 23, 26
decision-making, values as helping you
with, 111–113
deep breathing, as strategy for living with
anger, 55, 56–57
depression
    as blend of sadness and anger, 44
    clinical depression/major depressive
        disorder (MDD), 62
destructive angry acts, 54
disgust, 44
distress ("bad" stress), 69
dopamine, 118
DOTS (Distraction, Opting out, Thinking,
Substances and other strategies), 40–41
drives, as compared to emotions, 44
drugs, use of, 41, 60, 98, 100

E

eleutheromania (Greek language), 18
Ella's story, scenarios in her life, 9
embarrassment, 87
emojis and emoticons, 23
emotion chain reaction, 20
emotional intelligence

described, 2, 9
elements of, 9
how to strengthen yours, 14
as something to be learned, 10–11
emotional self-awareness
    benefits of, 9, 11, 12
    described, 2
    importance of, 6
    Will's experience with, 7
emotions. See also feelings; specific
    emotions
    anger as substitute emotion/cover-up
        emotion, 52–53
    as combinations of sensations,
        thoughts, and actions, 22–25
    defined, 19
    defining of, 18
    description of in languages other than
        English, 18, 19
    as having action tendencies, 38–39
    as helping you communicate, 26–27
    importance of, 1–2
    as messengers, 31–33, 45
    as moving you to act, 27
    myths and truths about, 27–28,
        47–48, 55, 61–62, 72, 80–81, 90, 100,
        119–120
    naming of, 35
    as not coming with a user's manual, 8
    as not controllable, 40
    origin of word, 21
    primary ones, 19, 44
    as providing focus, 26
    as providing information, 26, 36, 41,
        125, 127
    questions to help you understand them,
        34–41
    scientists' study of, 8–9
    why you have them, 25–27
empathy, 9
endorphins, 118
envy
    actions associated with, 79–80
    body sensations associated with, 78–79
    jealousy as related to, 75–76
    myths and truths about, 80–81
    role of, 76
    strategies for living with, 82–83
    thoughts associated with, 79
eudaemonia (happiness), 96

eustress (good stress), 69
The Expression of the Emotions in Man and Animals (Darwin), 23

F
facial expressions, 23
fear
    action tendency associated with, 38
    anxiety as different from, 68
    what it tells you, 46
feelings. *See also* emotions; *specific feelings*
    asking yourself what you are feeling, 34–36
    asking yourself what you can do with a feeling, 37–38
    asking yourself what your feeling is telling you, 36–38
    figuring out what to do with "bad" ones, 39, 41
    giving meaning to, 7
    giving names to, 7
fight-flight-or-freeze mode, 69, 77
Fisher, Helen (anthropologist), on experience of falling in love, 48–49
flow, values and, 116
focus
    emotions as helping you focus, 26
    values as giving you focus, 111
fortune-telling, as example of ANTs, 71

G
gigil (Tagalog language), 18
goals, as coming from values, 109–110
Grace's story, about dealing with anger, 51
guilt
    actions associated with, 89
    body sensations associated with, 88
    described, 86–87
    example of, 125–126
    myths and truths about, 90–91
    regret as cousin to, 92
    relationship with shame, 86
    strategies for living with, 91–92
    thoughts associated with, 88

H
happiness
    as joy, 95–102
    as ultimate positive feeling, 95

as well-being, 105–123
"happy hormones," 118
Harris, Russ (medical doctor), on DOTS, 40–41
Hartlin, Linda (psychologist), on behaviors caused by shame, 90
heaviness, feeling of, 88
hedonia (happiness), 96, 106
hedonistic/hedonism, 96, 98
hiding, as behavior caused by shame, 90
hormones
    adrenaline, 53
    dopamine, 118
    endorphins, 118
    "happy hormones," 118
    production of, 45, 49, 53
    release of stress hormones, 61, 89
    role of, 16, 45–46
    serotonin, 118
hotlines, 102
The How of Happiness (Lyubomirsky), 97

I
identity, building yours during teen years, 16
iktsuarpok (Inuit language), 18
Imani's story, about happiness as well-being, 105
information, emotions as providing, 26, 36, 41, 125, 127

J
Jason's story, about love, 43–44
jealousy
    actions associated with, 77–78
    body sensations associated with, 77
    dealing with, 37
    defined, 36
    myths and truths about, 80–81
    as related to envy, 75–76
    role of, 76
    strategies for living with, 81–82
    thoughts associated with, 77
    as trust buster, 77
joy
    actions associated with, 99
    body sensations associated with, 99
    defined, 97
    described, 97–98
    myths and truths about, 100

strategies for living with, 101–102
thoughts associated with, 99

K

L

M

N

O

P

Q

R

S

self-regulation, as one of five elements of emotional intelligence, 9
serotonin, 118
shame
    actions associated with, 90
    behaviors caused by, 90
    body sensations associated with, 89
    described, 86–88
    embarrassment as minor form of, 87
    myths and truths about, 90–91
    online shaming, 93
    relationship with guilt, 86
    strategies for living with, 93
    thoughts associated with, 89–90
Siddhartha Gautama (Buddha), on happiness, 96
social anxiety disorder, characteristics of, 39–40
social media
    shaming on, 93
    taking a break from as act of self-care, 120
social skills, as one of five elements of emotional intelligence, 9
stress
    "good" stress and "bad" stress, 69
    impact of on brain, 118–119
    relationship with anxiety, 68–69
suicide and crisis lifeline (988), 102
sukha (Sanskrit language), 18

T
teen years
    building your identity during, 16
    changes during, 15–17
    intense emotional experiences during, 5
    messages from adults about, 125
teenager, defined, 15
thoughts
    associated with anger, 53–54
    associated with anxiety, 70–71
    associated with envy, 79
    associated with guilt, 88
    associated with jealousy, 77
    associated with joy, 99
    associated with love, 46
    associated with sadness, 61
    associated with shame, 89–90
    associated with well-being, 118–119
    emotions as combination of sensations, thoughts, and actions, 22–25
    emotions as expressed through, 23–24
tizita (Amharic language), 18
Trey's story, about identifying feelings, 32–33
Tricia's story, about dealing with social anxiety, 113–115
trigger
    identification of, 35–36
    interpretation of, 21–22
    as part of emotion chain reaction, 20–21
trust, 77
Tyrell, debate team experience of, 107–108

V
values, personal
    described, 108–110
    and flow, 116
    and self-care, 117–118
    and well-being, 111–113
visualization, as strategy for living with anger, 57
voice, as conveying emotions, 23

W
warmlines, 102
well-being
    actions associated with, 119
    body sensations associated with, 118
    described, 106
    myths and truths about, 119–120
    strategies for living with, 120–123
    thoughts associated with, 118–119
    values and, 111–113
Will's story, about identifying feelings, 6–8

Y
yuan bei (Chinese language), 18

About the Author

Vidal Annan Jr., Ph.D., is a clinical psychologist who has worked with children, teens, and young adults for more than 15 years. As a clinician, Dr. Annan has extensive training in treatments that help individuals understand their thoughts and feelings better so they can make healthier choices in their personal, social, and professional lives. In addition to his clinical work,  Vidal enjoys presenting to audiences on topics related to mental health and wellness. He has also worked as a college professor, program director, and scientific researcher. He enjoys drawing, reading, watching sports, superhero movies, and hanging out with friends and family. He has two teenage children and constantly reminds them to listen to their feelings and live their values.